I am excited about Kevin Basconi's revelat
seer anointing and the gift of discernment.
gifts to start operating, to usher in the end t

SID ROTH
"It's Supernatural!"

I am honored and blessed to know Kevin and Kathy Basconi as friends and co-laborers in the ministry of sharing Jesus Christ with a lost and dying world. They not only walk in a high level of the gifts of the Spirit but they also have the fruit of the Spirit evident in their lives. Kevin's newest book, *Unlocking the Hidden Mysteries of the Seer Anointing*, will be a great blessing to anyone interested in learning and experiencing more of the seer realm.

DR. STEPHEN R. RICHARDSON
Ordained Foursquare minister and medical doctor, retired

This book will open your spiritual eyes and senses and catapult you into the realms of heaven that you never imagined was possible! Read this book if you are ready to activate the seer anointing in your life and go on an exciting supernatural journey that will radically change you life!

DAVID HERZOG
Author of Glory Invasion, www.thegloryzone.org

Kevin Basconi is a seer and has walked in this gift for many years. He is well qualified to write *Unlocking the Hidden Mysteries of the Seer Anointing*. For those of you who are hungry to learn more and to receive encouragement and impartation for the seer realms, then this book will be a blessing to you for sure.

PATRICIA KING
Founder XPMinistries, Xpmedia

Every time I read one of Kevin Basconi's books, I "see" spiritual gates opening up for those who have yet to enter into the invisible realm of God's glory. This book, is no exception. It will undoubtedly inspire you to reach your fullest potential in the Kingdom of God.

MICHAEL DANFORTH
Founder/Mountain Top International and SOHL. (school of higher learning)

After reading Kevin Basconi's first two books on *Dancing With Angels*, I invited him to come speak at our Methodist School for Supernatural Ministry. At the school he taught us about the ministry of angels and open heavens. During the school a number of the participants began to see angels at our center. And a number of us heard angels singing with us during an informal worship time. An open heaven was established at our center.

At a number of other events held at our center after the school with Kevin, people testified to seeing angels here even though we were not talking about angels at those events. The open heaven over our center remained. You will want to read about what Kevin has to say about corporate seer experiences in this, his latest book, *Unlocking the Hidden Mysteries of the Seer Anointing.* You will come to understand that the seer anointing and the ability to operate under an open heaven is not something limited to "special individuals." It is something available to all the sons and daughters of God.

REV. DR. FRANK BILLMAN
Director of Equipping Ministries at Aldersgate Renewal Ministries, Dean of the Methodist School for Supernatural Ministry, Adjunct Professor at United Theological Seminary for the Doctor of Ministry in Supernatural Ministry

Kevin Basconi has mastered the art of communicating at multiple levels in his writings. This book is presented first as a deeply confessional sharing of his personal journey into the "seer anointing" while at the same time giving a passionate plea for you, the reader, to move along with him on the same journey. At an even deeper level is the call and challenge to take up the mantle of the seer and begin your own journey into the prophetic. As you journey with him in this book, listen for the call of God on your own life and be ready to step into your destiny as a seer. Let the prayers of activation release the anointing of The Lord on your life and work! Let Kevin's amazing story of his own journey be the beginning of your journey. Don't just read the book! Pick up the mantle of the seer! Speak the prayers of activation aloud over yourself and let them open doors of revelation and wisdom to guide you into a deeper experience of the seer anointing.

PASTOR JAMES DURHAM
Higher Calling Ministries, Columbia South Carolina

As John was in the Spirit on the Lord's Day and both heard and saw from heaven's perspective, so believer's today must be able to see and hear in the Spirit in order to accomplish the great exploits reserved for this hour. This book will challenge you to go higher and reach further in the arena of the Spirit as you learn about the essentials of the seer anointing.

DAVID WHITE
Lead Pastor, The Gathering Church, Moravian Falls, NC

Kevin Basconi is a real seer. His new book is a great resource that can help you learn how to move in the seer anointing. What does that mean? There is an area that for all too long believers have not known about or were reluctant to experience themselves, a heavenly realm. We were designed to see and experience what is taking place in heaven right now! Today! Kevin knows the reality of this and has a God-given anointing to lead others into these kinds of supernatural experiences as well. Kevin has learned to see what literally is taking place in heaven and to communicate and teach others very clearly how they can operate in the seer anointing. Kevin gives numerous examples of how knowing what God has planned for you and what He is doing right now are both practical and essential for the day we live in. This book will give you realistic and intelligent insights and revelations about the seer realm. You will be encouraged, challenged, informed, inspired, and directed. You will walk away with an understanding of what Kevin has learned and be activated yourself to "see" what the Father is doing, just like Jesus (John 5:19)! I highly recommend this book!

ALAN KOCH
Senior Pastor Christ Triumphant Church, Lee's Summit, MO

*"To you it has been given
to know the mysteries
of the Kingdom of God."*

JESUS CHRIST

Unlocking the
Hidden Mysteries
of the
Seer
Anointing

Unlocking the
Hidden Mysteries
of the
Seer
Anointing

KEVIN BASCONI

This

book

Is

dedicated

to

God the Father, God the Son, and God the Holy Spirit

without

You

Guys

none

of

this

would

have

been

possible!

Table of Contents

Acknowledgments

I would like to acknowledge my precious wife, Kathleen (Kathy) Basconi. Without her prayers, support, and encouragement this book would not be possible. She has worked diligently for countless hours of reading and editing this material so that the reader would be encouraged and edified by this book. Besides knowing Jesus Christ as my personal Lord and Savior, Kathy is the most wonderful thing that has ever happened to me in my life!

Introduction

On Tuesday, August 28, 2012, at 7:38 a.m., I was in waiting on the Lord, seeking Him in prayer for the Moravian Falls School of the Seers. I was taken up into the heavenly realms. I came to a place that I had been before—the Sea of Glass Like Crystal. In the first book of my trilogy, *Dancing with Angels 1*, I write about the first time I was there.

It was Tuesday, May 28, 2002, and I was in the Talapia Hotel in Mwanza, Tanzania, Africa. I was taken up and landed on the shore of the Sea of Glass Like Crystal, which is made up of rubies, diamonds, sapphires, and other precious stones. I was lying there when Jesus came and stood over me. I witnessed hundreds of the angels of the Lord ascend and descend upon Jesus for several hours. Then the Lord Jesus began to teach me about the seer anointing.

In this second event I was not lying on the shore and Jesus was not standing over me. This time I was standing on the shore gazing out at the crystal clear waters. I was excited and grateful to be there, for it is such a beautiful place. As I watched a celestial sun (what appeared to be a sun; though I do not think there is a sun as we understand it in the heavenly realms) rose on the Sea of Glass Like Crystal and with it came an explosion of supernatural colors. Perhaps I was witnessing the glory of the Lord arising (Isaiah 60:1-2). These amazing colors released a spectacular light show that began to dance upon the perfectly still waters. The lights were reflecting the tangible glory of God in this marvelous plethora of colors between the sky and the sea. As I watched for a few moments, I knew that the Lord had brought me here for a purpose.

Just as this thought came into my mind, I heard a loud, whirring sound buzzing over me, kind of like a Huey helicopter. When it came in front of my eyes, I realized it was an angel, one like the cherubim I had seen before around the Father's throne in the heavenly realms. It was difficult to see the cherub clearly because he moved so fast that he appeared to be a blur of colors and glory. I could see his wings moving in sweeping circles that seemed to disperse the glory of God in all directions. I gazed at this angel as he flew around me for several moments. The sounds of his wings were amazing and very noisy. He moved acrobatically in the air around me like a human-sized hummingbird.

Suddenly this cherub flew directly in front of my eyes and stopped for an instant. At that moment I saw that his face was the face of a golden lion. The lion roared very loud and very clear. The force of the roar sent the hair on my head flying back as though a strong wind was blowing it. The glory of God came out of the lion's mouth and blew my hair back, and then the cherub took off again. I thought, *"That was amazing!"* I was standing there contemplating all that had happened when the cherub returned and flew directly in front of my eyes a second time. When he showed me his face this time, it was not the face of a lion but the face of an eagle.

The eagle was not a bald eagle but a golden eagle. The golden eagle lingered in front of me and gazed into my eyes for a moment. I saw this magnificent creature's pupils dilate as it seemed to gaze into the windows of my soul. Instantly I remembered what the Lord has taught me about the golden eagle. Golden eagles represent the seer anointing, which is a prophetic anointing of the mature prophet or mature believer in Christ. As this thought entered into my mind, the golden eagle shrieked. Again the force of the shriek blew my hair back. The cherub zoomed away into the heavenly realms dispersing the glory of God as it went! I began to wonder what all this meant.

Just then I felt someone touch me on the shoulder. As I turned around, I saw Jesus. He spoke to me and said, "The time has come for my people to arise. They will prophesy what they see. They shall roar like a golden lion. They will shriek like a golden eagle. When this happens the enemy will flee. Tell them the time has come to roar like a lion and to soar like an eagle—soaring to the highest heights of the heavenly realms where they will rise above the confusion and conflicts of the present world. From that place they will overcome the world and enter into My perfect will and the fullness of My rest. Tell them to soar into the heavenly realms and see what must take place after this." It's time for the body of Christ to roar and soar.

Another manifestation of the seer anointing happened when I was invited to the Methodist School of the Supernatural in Nashville to preach to the Methodist pastors about angelic ministry, the gift of discerning of spirits, and seer anointing. As I was praying before the meeting, I fell into a trance—a vision of the night. A well-known prophet in the body of Christ (representing the Holy Spirit) came to me in the vision and began to speak to me about the seer anointing. He was showing me how there is going to be a grace for activation and impartation of the seer realm. Sometimes when you are activated in the seer anointing, you can go forward into the future and sometimes you can go backwards into the past.

In the Methodist School of the Supernatural there were some pastors who thought I was the craziest, most absurd, and most unbiblical person that ever walked into one of their meetings. Through spiritual discernment, I knew that a certain cynical pastor in the back was especially bothered with those thoughts. So I prayed a little "heart's prayer": "*Lord, You open his eyes.*"

As I was ministering, a large angel stepped behind me. I always know when this angel comes because I begin to smell cinnamon, calamus, and myrrh and then the hair on my arms stands up. In the seer anointing you see with more than just your eyes. I knew this angel was there to release impartation.

I asked if anyone could see the angel that just stepped in behind me. No one responded. I told them that was OK and proceeded with my teaching. Later when we had a break, the pastor from the back of the room came up to me and said, "Can I talk to you?" His eyes were really big.

I told him, "Sure."

So he went on: "You know when you said an angel stepped behind you?"

"Yeah, I know," I responded.

He inhaled deeply and then exhaled the words: "I saw it!"

I smiled, "You did?"

He blurted out again, "I saw it!"

"What did he look like?" I asked him.

He went on to tell me about the angel: "He was about nine foot tall, he had on a white robe, he had a sword, he had blue eyes..." He described him to a T.

I said, "Oh! Isn't God wonderful?"

If God activated the seer anointing in this skeptical pastor's life, then God can certainly activate the seer anointing in your life. The pastor did not believe it was possible. He did not believe in the seer anointing theologically. But when He came to a certain place, God in His sovereignty opened this cynical pastor's spiritual eyes to "see." So, God in His sovereignty can certainly release a spiritual activation to see and to discern into your life too!

I encourage you to pray the following prayer of activation out loud from a kneeling position.

Prayer of Preparation

Father, in the mighty name of Jesus Christ of Nazareth, I ask You today to send the Holy Spirit to guide me and to teach me about Your Kingdom. Lord, I am asking You for understanding and wisdom about Your nature and Your Kingdom. I am asking for Your good gifts, Father, and I am asking that You would begin to reveal the hidden mysteries of Your Kingdom to me. Reveal them to my spirit, God.

Lord, I ask that you open my eyes to see and open my mind to comprehend what Your word really says. Lord, reveal to me the gospel, the truth of Your word in this hour. Lord, I ask that You would open the eyes of my understanding and the eyes of my spirit man. Activate the eyes of my heart. Father, I thank You for the precious blood of Jesus and I cover myself in it. Lord, I ask that You would forgive me for anything that I've done, for anything that I've said, and for any area my spirit, mind, or heart that has been unacceptable in Your sight. Lord, please forgive my unbelief and help me to believe and to understand the reality of what Your word truly says—not what I think that it is supposed to say or what I've have been incorrectly taught that Your word says.

Lord, I thank You that the Kingdom of Heaven is already within me. Lord, I ask You to help me to understand Your Kingdom and that Your Kingdom is a supernatural place. And I thank You that I am already a citizen of light. I am Your child; and I ask You, Father, that You would give me Your good gifts today. Lord, I ask for wisdom and understanding. I thank You that You are going to release wisdom and revelation about You, about Your Kingdom, about the Holy Spirit, about the gifts of the Spirit, and about the supernatural dynamics in Your created realm. Lord, I thank You for the supernatural DNA that You have placed within me by Your Spirit.

Lord, I give You the praise and the honor and the glory for all of these things. I pray in Jesus' mighty name. Amen.

CHAPTER 1

What Is the Seer Anointing?

I want to start developing our understanding of the seer anointing by building a scriptural foundation and looking at the Holy Scriptures in great detail concerning the seer anointing. If you are reading this, you are a seer. It's not about being a chosen vessel any longer. Why? Because you are created in the very image of God. Once you come into the family of God—what most of the church calls being born again—your spiritual, God-given DNA is activated.

Jesus referred to being "born again" in John 3:7. The literal meaning of the Greek word is "born from above," "to be reborn from the heavenly realms," or "to be reborn from the spirit."

We see our spiritual DNA in Genesis chapter 1: "*And God said, '**See**, I have given you every herb that yields seed which is on the face of all the earth, and every tree whose fruit yields seed; to you it shall be for food. Also, to every beast of the earth, to every bird of the air, and to everything that creeps on the earth, in which there is life, I have given every green herb for food'; and it was so. Then **God saw** everything that He had made, and indeed it was very good. So the evening and the morning were the sixth day*" (Genesis 1:29-31, emphasis added).

What I want you to notice is that "God saw." The Creator is a seer. I find it amazing that the Creator of heaven and earth, Elohim, created you and me in His image to be seers too. And one of the first things He told humans to do is to "see." Of course in Genesis 1:28 the Lord also instructed you and me to "*be fruitful and multiply; fill the earth and subdue it; have dominion.*" This was made possible in part by

God's grace and activation of the human race to see into both the temporal and spiritual realms. So the next thing the Lord instructed us to do was to "see." And that's your spiritual DNA. You are created to be a seer, to have intimacy and communion with God.

God Is a Seer

As you read some more in Genesis 1, try to look at these familiar passages of Scripture with an open heart. Sometimes when we look at a passage of Scripture we know, we tune out because we already know what it says. But sometimes we *really* don't know what it says. We know what we've been taught it says or we know what we think it says, but we don't have the true revelation of what it actually says. Many of us do not actually have a true revelation of the Gospel.

> *In the beginning God created the heavens and the earth. The earth was without form, and void; and darkness on the face of the deep. And the Spirit of **God was hovering** over the face of the waters* (Genesis 1:1-2, emphasis added).

The Spirit of God *hovering* was the glory. When we praise until the glory comes and we worship in the glory and we stand in the glory, there is a grace and an anointing for creative things to happen: creative miracles like deaf ears opening, creative miracles like people having money in their wallets multiply, creative miracles like dental miracles. These kinds of creative miracles, signs, and wonders are an element of the seer realm.

> *Then God said, "Let there be light"; and there was light* (Genesis 1:3).

Did you ever wonder why the first thing God made was light? Because you can't see without light.

> *And **God saw** the light, that it was good; and God divided the light from the darkness. God called the light Day, and the darkness He called Night. So the evening and the morning were the first day* (Genesis 1:4-5, emphasis added).

In verse 4 it tells us "God saw"; He was a seer.

Then God said, "Let there be a firmament in the midst of the waters, and let it divide the waters from the waters." Thus God made the firmament, and divided the waters which were under the firmament from the waters which were above the firmament; and it was so. And God called the firmament **Heaven***. So the evening and the morning were the second day. Then God said, "Let the waters under the heavens be gathered together into one place, and let the dry land appear"; and it was so. And God called the dry land* **Earth***, and the gathering together of the waters He called Seas. And* **God saw** *that it was good* (Genesis 1:6-10, emphasis added).

God created two realms: a spiritual or heavenly realm and a temporal or earthly realm that we walk and breathe in.

Then God said, "Let the earth bring forth grass, the herb that yields seed, and the fruit tree that yields fruit according to its kind, whose seed is in itself, on the earth"; and it was so. And the earth brought forth grass, the herb that **yields seed according to its kind***, and the tree that yields fruit, whose* **seed** *is in itself* **according to its kind***. And* **God saw** *that it was good. So the evening and the morning were the third day* (Genesis 1:11-13, emphasis added).

When we sow seed, it brings forth according to its kind (see Galatians 6:7-8). It is a spiritual principal that we see first at Creation. For instance, if you sow into the seer anointing, you will get the seer anointing; if you sow into the glory, the glory is going to come upon you. So when you find a ministry that has what you want, sow into that ministry.

Then God said, "Let there be lights in the firmament of the heavens to divide the day from the night; and let them be for signs and seasons, and for days and years; and let them be for lights in the firmament of the heavens to give light on the *earth"; and it was so. Then God made two great lights: the greater light to rule the day, and the lesser light to rule the night. He made the stars also. God set them in the firmament of the heavens to give light on the earth, and to rule over the day and over the night, and to divide the light from the darkness. And **God saw** that it was good* (Genesis 1:14-18, emphasis added).

In verse 21, after God created the sea creatures and the birds, we find: *"And **God saw** that it was good"* (emphasis added). After God created the beasts and creeping things on the earth, it tells us in verse 25 that *"**God saw** that it was good"* (emphasis added). So far we have five instances in chapter 1 of Genesis where *"**God saw.**"* Now let's continue to learn more about your God given spiritual DNA to be a seer.

CHAPTER 2

Your Spiritual DNA

The narrative then goes to the creation of mankind and God's instructions to him.

In verse 26 the Bible tells us, "*Then God said, 'Let Us make man in **Our** image, according to **Our** likeness'*" (emphasis added).The capitalized "Our" is referring to the Trinity: God the Father, God the Son, and God the Holy Spirit. God is a three-part being and we are created in His image; we have three parts, which we will discuss later. We are created in God's image and so we have God's spiritual DNA. Therefore, because God sees, we are created to see.

Verse 26 goes on to tell us more of God's discussion about His creation: "*Let them have dominion over the fish of the sea, over the birds of the air, and over the cattle, over all the earth and over every creeping thing that creeps on the earth.*" The Scriptures then reflect on mankind's creation in verse 27: "*So God created man in His own image; in the image of God He created him; male and female He created them.*" In verse 28 God begins to relate to His creation: "*Then God blessed them, and God said to them, 'Be fruitful and multiply; fill the earth and subdue it; have dominion over the fish of the sea, over the birds of the air, and over every living thing that moves on the earth.'*"

The next instruction God gives to mankind is the admonition to "see": "*And God said, '**See**, I have given you every herb that yields seed which is on the face of all the earth, and every tree whose fruit yields seed; to you it shall be for food'*" (verse 29, emphasis added).

Finally in verse 31 we have the conclusion of this dynamic: "*Then God saw everything that He had made, and indeed it was very good. So the evening and the morning were the sixth day*" (emphasis added).

Up to this point we find that "God saw" six times; but here in verse 31, when God **sees** this seventh time that man is good, it is particularly important. The seventh time prophetically means completion, perfection, or rest. God created the whole universe so that we could interact with Him. One of the ways we can do this is to see, not just seeing with our eyes. When God created the universe, He saw that it was good. And one of the first things God told His creation, man, to do was to see. The Creator of the heavens and earth wants for you to see and discern spiritually.

What does the enemy of our soul want to do? He wants to hamper us from having a relationship with God. And if God's purpose for us is to see, the enemy diligently works to make us spiritually blind and deaf. The enemy hates the seer anointing and seeks to keep God's people from stepping into this supernatural realm. The enemy knows that when we do begin to see and hear in the spiritual realms we will be empowered to manifest the Kingdom of Heaven in our sphere of influence. This is a great threat to his plans of deception and uncovers his lies.

You are created in God's very image to have a supernatural spiritual DNA to see—to be a seer. That's how God created you. The Creator of heaven and earth created you to see, not only in the natural realm but through the finished work of Christ on the tree of Calvary you can also see into the spiritual realm. That is what is often referred to as the seer anointing.

Place your hand on your chest and say: "*I am a seer. I am created in God's very image. I am good. I am supposed to see into God and I am supposed to see into God's spiritual Kingdom. That privilege is my spiritual inheritance through the finished work of Christ's on the Cross.*"

God is a triune being and we are created in His very image. We are created with a spirit, a soul, and a body. So the reason why most of us, Christians and non-Christians, don't see and hear more clearly from the spiritual realm is because the god of this world has blinded our spiritual eyes. With the activation of the seer anointing, we will break through that blindness and begin to see.

As I have written in my trilogy of books, *The Reality of Angelic Ministry Today*, the activation of the seer anointing or supernatural encounters can manifest or transpire in one of two realms: (1) the temporal realm, which is the earth, or (2) the spiritual realm, which is heavenly, both of which we just read that God created. We also read that God created us to see. Because we are created in God's image, we can see into both realms—the spiritual realm and the temporal or carnal realm.

Remember that we are created in God's image to be seers.

God Is a Spirit

John 4:24 tells us, "*God is Spirit, and those who worship Him must worship in spirit and truth.*" The Lord created each of us to worship Him. It is important to see God to worship Him. And this fact brings us to a very important aspect of the seer anointing.

The seer anointing is much more than seeing in the spirit and it's much more than seeing an angel with your eyes or vision, as important and wonderful as that may be. When your spiritual DNA is activated, you will not only see with your eyes but you will also discern with your spiritual senses as well. And the eyes of your understanding will become enlightened.

You begin to taste, you begin to touch, you begin to hear, you begin to smell, and you begin to see into the spiritual realm to discern things both good and evil. And remember that the Lord gave you dominion over all of those things.

Some people are afraid to see into the spiritual realm because they may see a demon. God has given you all authority and power over every living thing upon the earth (see Genesis 1:28; Luke 9:1). The devil is under our feet (Romans 16:20); we have dominion over him. When demons show up, you have the power and the jurisdiction to rebuke them and to take authority over them and tell them to get out of the way. Just rebuke demons in the power of the name of Jesus Christ of Nazareth and send them to the abyss.

Be aware that the seer anointing is not something to take lightly. It is a weightier thing, because when God opens your eyes to see or discern angels or demons, there is a purpose for it—for you to recreate Christ in your sphere of influence. We are created in the likeness of Christ. Jesus said the works that He did, we would do the same way Jesus did them (see John 14:12).

Remember, God is a triune being and we are created in His very image, so we are created with a spirit, a soul, and a body. Paul understood our true nature as triune beings. Paul also understood why developing the gift of discerning of spirits in our lives is crucial to living a triumphant life in Christ. Look at Paul's prayer for the church to have the seer anointing activated in their lives.

Understanding Your Spiritual Eyes and Unlocking Your Spiritual Vision

We find Paul's apostolic prayer in Ephesians, chapter 1. This prayer deals directly with your spiritual eyes. As you read these scriptures, there is something being activated in your spirit to hear and to see.

> *I do not cease to give thanks for you, making mention of you in my prayers: that the God of our Lord Jesus Christ, the Father of glory, may give to you the spirit of wisdom and revelation in the knowledge of Him, the eyes of your understanding being enlightened; that you may know what is the hope of His calling, what are the riches of the glory of His inheritance in the saints* (Ephesians 1:16-18).

Put your hand on your chest and say: "*The Father of glory has given me an inheritance, and I am the Father's inheritance. I am created in His image to be a seer. Lord, thank You for opening up my spiritual eyes to see. Amen!*"

To see what? Verse 19 goes on to tell us: "*What is the exceeding greatness of His power toward us who believe, according to the working of His mighty power.*" The Greek words translated "mighty power" are *ischus* and *dunamis*, which we will talk more about later.

Paul goes on in verses 20 through 22 to say, *"Which He worked in Christ when He raised Him from the dead and seated Him at His right hand in the heavenly places, far above all principality and power and might and dominion, and every name that is named, not only in this age but also in that which is to come. And He put all things under His feet."* Where are all things? Say, "All things are under my feet." Verses 22 and 23 go on to say, *"And gave Him to be head over all things to the church, which is His body, the fullness of Him who fills all in all."*

Ask the Lord to do this in you: *"Lord, fill me with all in all."*

I encourage you to pray the whole prayer from Ephesians 1:16-23 over your spirit, soul, and body every day when you rise up and lie down for the rest of your life. Your triune nature—spirit, soul, and body—can be activated by praying, by reading or hearing anointed teaching, by just sitting under the anointing, by resting in God's tangible glory, or by reading or hearing testimonies of seer experiences. There are amazing testimonies in my trilogy of books, *The Reality of Angelic Ministry Today.* We have received dozens of testimonies from people who have their spiritual eyes activated to see and hear into the spiritual realm as they have read the trilogy.

Sometimes you need to be exposed to others and their experiences; then the seed they have is planted into you and brings forth godly fruit after its own kind. If you want the seer anointing, sow into the ministries that operate in the seer anointing. You need to get around people that operate under the seer anointing. I encourage you to get CDs and other teachings about the seer anointing and listen to them, even play them at night when you are sleeping. Sometimes your human spirit is more open to receive spiritual things when you are asleep.

So let's continue to lay a foundation for the activation of the seer anointing in fullness.

We can have seer experiences in the spiritual realm or we can have supernatural experiences (the seer anointing activated in our lives) in the earthly or world or temporal realm—the natural realm that we live in. We contact that realm with our five carnal senses.

We can say that we interact with the world or temporal realm through our soul, which is made up of our mind, will, and emotions. We also relate to the earthly realm or the earthly environment through our body, which is also our flesh. Remember that God created us in His image with three parts: spirit, soul, and body.

In our everyday earthly life, usually our soul—our mind, will, and emotions—guides us and our flesh propels us. We respond to the needs in our flesh—clothing, food, shelter, etc. Most Christians never go beyond that; they are what the Apostle Paul calls carnal Christians or immature Christians (see 1 Corinthians 3:1). Jesus wants us to be led by our spirits. He wants us to be so intimately in tune with the Holy Spirit that we will do whatever He says whenever He says it. He wants us to become eagles so we can soar.

As we press into the Kingdom of God, we will begin to experience segments of time when our spirit will become dominant in terms of our perception. At these times we can experience the supernatural realm more readily than the carnal realm. Our spiritual senses will become activated, and we can discern things in the spirit more clearly than we can from our temporal senses—what scientists call the five traditional senses of the human being. It can happen for a couple of seconds, it can happen for a couple of minutes, or it can happen for longer periods of time. There was a season in my life where it happened for about nine months. Everywhere I went I could see angels and demons. Every day I would go up into heaven.

Maybe you would like to have some of these supernatural experiences. You need to press into the Kingdom of God. When I say this, I am referring to seeking the Lord with all your heart, all your soul, and all your mind.

When we do seek the Lord with all of our spirit, soul, and bodies, the Lord promises that we *will* find Him (see Deuteronomy 4:29).

God's Promises to You

There are some promises given to us in Scripture where God makes wonderful proclamations that we can use to activate our spiritual senses. One example is in Jeremiah 29:11-14:

For I know the thoughts that I think toward you, says the Lord,
thoughts of peace and not of evil, to give you a future and a
hope. Then you will call upon Me and go and pray to Me, and I
will listen to you. And you will seek Me and find Me, when you
search for Me with all your heart. I will be found by you, says
the Lord, and I will bring you back from your captivity; I will
gather you from all the nations and from all the places where
I have driven you, says the Lord, and I will bring you to the
place from which I cause you to be carried away captive.

(In Jeremiah's time the place of captivity was Babylon. Now, prophetically, we can accurately say that captivity is bondage to the enemy through sin and deception.)

I had a personal experience with Jesus pertaining to the preceding scriptures when He appeared to me November 25, 2001. He walked up to me, put His eyes close to mine, and He said, "I have good thoughts for you, not evil, to give you a future and a hope; and when you seek Me, you will find Me when you search for Me with all your heart." Then He touched my hand and it felt like warm oil pouring down and off of my left elbow.

From that day on for nine months, almost everywhere I looked I saw or discerned angels and demons. And the presence of the Holy Spirit—the communion, the koinonia of the Holy Spirit—was with me everywhere I went. At times people would walk into my little house located in a crack neighborhood. When they opened the door and stepped over the threshold, they would go out in the spirit. The glory and presence of God was so strong in that little house that people would be slain in the spirit (fall unconscious) by the power of God's presence. Why? Because I sought God's Kingdom violently!

I pressed into the Kingdom of God and sought to grow closer to the Lord, asking Him to open the eyes of my spirit. The Lord tells us that when we call upon Him and we pray, He will listen to us; and when we seek Him, He will find us. That's a promise for all of us. It is a promise for you too! In the next chapter we will look at several keys that can help you develop your ability to press into the Kingdom of God violently!

CHAPTER 3

Seek First the Kingdom

Matthew 6:33 tells us, *"But seek first the kingdom of God and His righteousness, and all these things shall be added to you."* What things? *All*!

When I first saw this one I really dug in; because when I had that experience where Jesus came down and talked to me face-to-face as a man does to a friend (see Exodus 33:11), He touched my hand and He called me to the nations. I was the guy who had been struggling with drug addiction for decades. For a short time I was basically living in the street. I didn't have a place to call home. I didn't have any money, I was in debt, I had a herniated disk in my back, I had deafness in my ears, and I had a blood disease. Now I hear almost perfectly and my back is completely healed. God supernaturally took me from sickness to health, from poverty to prosperity, and He launched me out into the nations—thirty-three nations as of this writing—preaching the gospel of the Kingdom.

How did that happen? I stepped out of the carnal realm and into the spiritual realm where I had an encounter with Christ by pressing into His Kingdom. Seer experiences—supernatural experiences— are more real than the clothing you are wearing right now. That's what's going to release you into your destiny.

You may have your destiny on hold. Have you ever been on a trip and are at the airport but your plane has been delayed? Sometimes you even have to stay overnight because your plane is delayed. I declare right now that you *will* take off, that you *will* step into your destiny. It's not too late. The devil wants to tell you it's too late; but it's *not* too late. It's not too late for you to step into your God-ordained destiny. Part of what you need is to understand the seer anointing and to learn how to step into the reality of the seer realms and to activate them in your life.

These words in John 14:21 are the words of Jesus Christ Himself: *"He who has My commandments and keeps them, it is he who loves Me. And he who loves Me will be loved by My Father, and I will love him and manifest Myself to him."* The word *manifest* is translated from a Greek word that means "to appear in person" or "to display plainly" like a fine work of art. When we love God, when we keep His commandments, basically Jesus has promised to come and have tea with us. (That's a nice thought, isn't it?) In the introduction I wrote about a wonderful supernatural seer experience in which I was taken up into heaven and saw a cherub flying around me. I saw the head of the lion and the head of the golden eagle. But the most amazing and wonderful part of that experience was when Jesus came to me and put His hands on my shoulders and spoke to me and gave me revelation of what I was seeing.

A Prophetic Promise for You

I prophesy that you are going to be activated to soar and roar.

Does it make sense in the natural realm? Don't think about it in the natural realm. Think about it from the spiritual realm—having your spirit man become dominant in terms of your perception. Have you ever had an incident when you had a ball of light fly by and you thought that it might be an angel? Guess what? It *is* an angel. Have you ever had the sense that someone else is in the car with you? Guess what? Somebody *is* in the car with you. Sometimes it's Jesus. Sometimes when you "feel like" something is happening, *it is!*

We find an even better prophecy in Revelation 19:10: *"For the testimony of Jesus is the spirit of prophecy."* There will be instances and periods when the Lord will call many of us to storm the gates of heaven and to take the Kingdom by force. This is what I mean when I speak of "pressing in." Really it is just a matter of allowing the Holy

Spirit to develop a holy hunger within you. You can't do it from your soul, but you can pray and ask God to give you a holy hunger.

You can purpose in your heart right now: *"I am going to press into the Kingdom. There is a destiny for me. There is a supernatural release and activation that God is going to place on my life as I read this book. I am going to catch something and I am going to receive an impartation of the seer anointing."*

Paul prayed for a lot of people for impartation. He felt it was very important. In Romans 1:11 he said, *"For I long to see you, that I may impart to you some spiritual gift, so that you may be established."* You can receive impartation where you are sitting right now. The more you read and the more you are around people who have the spiritual gifts of the Holy Spirit that you desire, the more that impartation has a chance to build, strengthen, and be released into your life. At times, impartation is better *"caught than taught."*

Listen to the word of God because the word is alive, the word is living. There is power and anointing in God's words. The Holy Spirit rests upon God's word. According to Psalm 103:20, God's angels heed His word to perform it. Do you know what that means? When you hear a prophetic word spoken or see something in the Bible you know is for you, you can remind God: "Lord, *he said*...." Or, "Lord, *You said* in Your word...." Then go on to tell God, "So, Father, I believe that word and I release Your angels to go forth and bring that to pass in my life. In John 14:14 Jesus encourages you and me by promising: *"If you ask anything in My name, I will do it."*

The spiritual realm is much more real than anything that we know in this world. Hebrews 11:1-3 tells us, *"Now faith is the substance of things hoped for, the evidence of things not seen. For by it the elders obtained a good testimony. By faith we understand that the worlds were framed by the word of God."* So, as you hear the word of God being spoken or read the words in Scripture or read testimonies in God-breathed books, something is being framed in your sphere of influence. A supernatural door or gate of breakthrough is open to you in the spiritual realm, in the seer realm. Go through, go through the gate! (See 2 Samuel 5:20; Micah 2:13; Isaiah 40:3; Isaiah 42:16.)

As you hear or read testimonies, you have an opportunity to step into something that hasn't manifested yet in your life. You may be called to be a missionary and yet you have never left American soil. You may be called to lead 100 or 200 thousand people to Christ and yet you haven't even led 100 yet. But there is a grace for you to step into God's preordained destiny right now.

Hebrews 11:3-4 tells us: "*By faith we understand that the worlds were framed by the word of God so that the things which are seen were not made of things which are visible. By faith Abel offered to God a more excellent sacrifice than Cain, through which he obtained witness that he was righteous, God testifying of his gifts; and through it he being dead still speaks.*"

Sometimes you need to sow seed that is acceptable to God. One way of activating promises and callings that are not yet manifest in your life can come by giving and sowing your first fruits to God. What does that look like? We need to follow the example of the Hebrews who celebrate Rosh Chodesh at the beginning of each month. We would come before God and give Him our first fruits. It is a time of celebration and a time of worship where we love on God, we love on Abba Father, and we give Him our best, our first fruits.

I give Him my first fruits every day. I get down on my knees and pray, "*Lord, I come before You this morning and I thank You, the Father of my Lord Jesus Christ. I bow my knees to You and I ask that You would grant to me according to the riches of Your glory that I might be filled with all the fullness of God, that I might be able to comprehend with all of the saints what is the length and depth and breadth and height and to personally know the love of Christ.*"

Sometimes we sow supernatural seed by simply giving God our time. That is not a very complicated key, is it? First fruits are not always monetary but there are times when we begin to give that God recognizes our offering. It's important to give Him what He wants from us. Seek the Lord in this individually. I share more basic teaching about the importance of Rosh Chodesh and giving first fruits to the Lord on a monthly basis in my book *The Sword of the Lord and the Rest of the Lord.*

The Scriptures also tell us that we can violently seek the Kingdom of God. That is what literally launched me into these heavenly realms of Christ's Kingdom. In the next chapter we will look at more keys that can help unlock the hidden mysteries of the seer anointing and enable you to discern the heavenly realms.

CHAPTER 4

Take the Kingdom by Force

Matthew 11:12 illustrates taking the Kingdom by force: "*And from the days of John the Baptist until now the kingdom of heaven suffers violence, and the violent take it by force.*" Sometimes you need to take the Kingdom of Heaven by force! As a new believer it was my passion and hunger to know Jesus Christ in a more intimate and tangible way. Your passion and hunger can also open the door of the heavens to you too. I believe that anyone can have the seer anointing activated in their lives and have supernatural experiences.

Anyone can learn to see into the spirit. Yes, I said *learn* to see. Really it is just retraining your triune nature and exercising your spiritual senses to have your spirit become dominate in terms of your perception. This can be a process, and we will be looking at this in more detail. So begin to press into the teachings and the anointing of the Holy Spirit that will be released through this book. You can catch something! The anointing or the gift to see can rub off on you. You can activate the seer anointing in your life by just embracing the atmosphere of this book. Again, let me encourage you to press in. It is even possible that the testimonies in my books will become prophetic words for you according to the scriptural principle of Revelation 19:10: "*The testimony of Jesus is the spirit of prophecy.*" Many people contact us and testify to having their spiritual eyes activated or opened as they have read the books. This same type of supernatural activation can happen to you as you read this book too. Just believe to receive! Pray this short prayer now:

Father, I choose to believe to receive Your Kingdom as I read this book. I choose to take the Kingdom of Heaven by force, and I accept that this book is a prophetic promise for me. Lord, as I read the scriptures in this book, I ask that You would breathe on them by Your Spirit. Lord, I thank You that You are opening the eyes of my understanding, and that my spiritual senses are becoming enlightened to discern from the realms of heaven with all five of my senses. Thank You, Lord, that I will begin to see, hear, smell, touch, taste, and discern attributes from the Kingdom of Heaven. In Jesus name I pray. Amen.

Discovering Your True Nature in Christ

Remember, we are *created in the very image of Jesus*, the Creator of the heavens and the earth. We saw this in Genesis 1:26: *"Then God said, 'Let Us make man in Our image, according to Our likeness.'"* The Bible clearly teaches us that God is a spiritual being who is made up of three parts. This aspect of the Lord's nature, commonly referred to as the Trinity, is composed of God the Father, God the Son, and God the Holy Spirit.

Likewise you are also created by the Lord as a triune being. You have a spirit, a soul, and a body.

The Apostle Paul understood this three-part composition of human beings and encourages believers in the Messiah to yield to their true nature. Paul said in Galatians 1:11-12, *"That the gospel which was preached by me is not according to man. For I neither received it from man, nor was I taught it, but it came through the revelation of Jesus Christ."* Paul was in the Arabian Desert when Jesus came and taught him the gospel. He got the gospel by revelation. He had visitations of Jesus. It is well-documented in Scripture that he had several visitations of Jesus. Paul had visitations of Jesus where he received both wisdom and revelation. One of the things he received supernatural understanding of was our triune nature and the need for the Body of Christ to step into the spiritual realm. Paul prays that we can know that we too can see, hear, taste, smell, and understand things from the spiritual realm and that these spiritual things are more real than the natural or temporal realm.

Let's look at this admonition of Paul's teaching in connection with this dynamic of our spiritual nature in 1 Thessalonians 5:23: *"Now may the God of peace Himself sanctify you completely* [perfect in every respect]*; and may your whole spirit, soul, and body be preserved* [to be guarded from loss or injury by keeping an eye on one closely, to guard, to fortify, to fulfill a prophetic word or command of God, to keep custody over an individual, or to keep them pure and undefiled] *blameless at the coming* [perusia] *of our Lord Jesus Christ."*

If you want to step into the seer realm, holiness is not an option. We must walk in holiness. In Paul's prayer here—*"may your whole spirit, soul, and body be preserved blameless"*—he is talking about our nature. Remember Genesis 1: *"Then God said, 'Let Us make man in Our image.'"* That's God the Father, God the Son, and God the Holy Spirit. We are created with a spirit, a soul, and a body. So if we are going to understand the seer anointing, we need to understand what that characteristic of our true nature looks like.

We all have a spirit. The Greek word for "spirit" is *pneuma*. It means a spirit, our spirit, or the Holy Spirit. So when we were created in God's image, a little piece of Papa God was put in us. Our spirit is the "real" person of our existence, and it is our spirit that is regenerated or "born again" at the moment that we pray to receive the salvation of the Messiah. Remember, "born again" means we are "born from above" or born from heavenly realms. It is this born-again spirit that we want to become dominant in our lives. God wants us to be transformed from the inside out.

We all have a soul: *"May your whole spirit, **soul**, and body be preserved blameless."* The Greek word for "soul" is *psuche*, the same Greek word from which we get *psychology*. Our soul is made up of our mind, will, and emotions.

We all have a body, too: *"May your whole spirit, soul, and **body** be preserved blameless."* The Greek word for "body" is *soma*, which means body, outer man, whole body, or flesh.

The enemy will try to oppress you or to keep you from stepping into your God-ordained destiny in one of two ways: (1) He wants to put sickness or affliction on your body. (2) He also can put yokes of darkness upon your soul. Sometimes this takes the form of depression, mental illness, emotional distress, sadness, or other mental conditions (these are all issues of the soul). The bottom line is that the enemy wants to rob your supernatural destiny. Paul understood this. He understood that we were created with a triune nature. Scripture tells us that you were knit together in your mother's womb by the hand of God (Psalm 139:13, NIV). (See also Jeremiah 1:5.) God's perfect plan for each of us is to live in perfect peace and to have abundant life (Isaiah 26:3; John 10:10).

Our spirit is at the core of our being. Your spirit is the "real you," and it is your spirit that is actually "born again." The spirit and the soul are interchangeable at times and they are similar and intertwined; but when we are "born again," it is not that our "soul is saved," as some Christians say, but it is our spirit that is saved. I challenge you to search the Scriptures and believe them because of what they say, not according to what you've been taught or what you have misguidedly and erroneously believed.

Our spirit is our real man. Our spirit is what will live on in eternity with Christ in heaven. Sometimes when we step into the seer realm and begin to see angels and begin to see into the spiritual realm, what happens is that our spirit becomes dominant in terms of perception.

Many people struggle through life. The primary reason for this is that we live our lives by allowing our soul to dominate our daily activities and choices. As we are led by our soul, many times we make very poor choices and sinful decisions. Sin opens the door for the enemy to place yokes of darkness and oppression upon our lives (upon our body and within our soul). In other words, we allow our soul (intellect or mind, will, and emotions) to rule and reign in our daily lives and day-to-day decisions. That's why we can't step into the spirit because we are led by our soul. (To learn how you can set yourself free from yokes of darkness and demonic oppression, listen to my teaching *Overcoming Yokes of Darkness and Demonic Oppression,* available in our online book store.)

We all have a body, which is our flesh. Most people in the world are ruled by their carnal or fleshly desires. We all have basic needs each day such as food, clothing, and shelter. These carnal desires of our flesh are a powerful driving force behind most human beings' lives. This is true for the majority of Christians too. Most born-again people never really achieve the victory that the Messiah purchased for us on the Cross, because we don't let our spirit become dominant in our daily activities. Few of us are in reality led by our spirit consistently.

By reading and receiving the information and anointing in this book, I pray that your spirit will become dominant in terms of perception and this will transform your life. The Apostle Paul referred to Christians who were operating in the soulish and fleshly realms as "carnal" Christians (1 Corinthians 3:1, 3-4; Romans 8:6). In other words, people can receive Jesus Christ as Savior and yet never really mature into the fullness of the Christ's salvation. In the next chapter we will activate several scriptural principles that will empower us to grow into mature sons and daughters of the Most High God.

CHAPTER 5

Overcoming Carnal Christianity

Paul speaks about carnal Christians in 1 Corinthians 3:1-4. In verse 1 he says, *"Brothers, I could not speak to you* [teach you the weightier matters of the Kingdom] *as to spiritual people but as to carnal, as to babes in Christ."* In other words, he could not teach them the deeper things of God. In order to receive the weightier matters of God, your spirit has to receive them. You have to bypass your mind (intellect). You may also find it necessary to overcome the ungodly mindsets and unbiblical doctrines you've heard and religious dogma that you've been taught. All of these things may have become what Paul calls "strongholds" within your spirit (2 Corinthians 10:4).

If you have hope that God will activate you to see, hope is good; but you need to overcome these strongholds. For example, believing, "God would use the pastor to see but not me," or, "God would use the evangelist for those things but not me," are mental strongholds. It's not so much that you've been taught that, but it may have been demonstrated and insinuated to you in the Body of Christ throughout your walk with God. So, without an unbiblical idea being spoken or taught to you from the pulpit, such a stronghold can subconsciously become an ungodly belief that you have grown to incorrectly accept as gospel. You need to overcome those strongholds. These mental strongholds can also be rightly called ungodly beliefs. Unfortunately, many of God's people live with ungodly beliefs. But the Lord is seeking to transform our minds and renew them with Christ-like minds.

As we saw in 1 Thessalonians 5:23, Paul encourages us to be sanctified completely, spirit, soul, and body. Paul clearly delineates between these three aspects of our created nature. We don't hear this often; we need to teach the word. We need to allow the precious Holy Spirit to transform us. The Scriptures tell us that we need to seek to have our minds (our souls) renewed, transformed, or sanctified (see Romans 12:2). Here is what I believe: our soul is not saved when we are born again; it's our spirit that is saved. Some people never walk into the deeper things of God because their soul is never fully changed. They never submit to the transforming work of the Holy Spirit or renew their mind by diligently studying God's word.

Activating Your Spiritual Transformation

Paul understood our triune nature; he understood we are a three-part being. Ephesians 4:22-24 outlines this Kingdom dynamic for us: *"Put off your former conduct, the old man which grows corrupt according to the deceitful lusts* [your flesh], *and be renewed in the spirit of your mind, and that you put on the new man which was created according to God, in true righteousness and holiness."*

So whose responsibility is it to renew your mind? Yours. How do you do it? One way is to exercise your spiritual senses by reason of use to have your mind renewed (see Hebrews 5:14). This Scripture tells us that it is our responsibility to overcome or to put off the corrupt conduct, deceitful nature, and the lusts that were evident in our flesh. We are made up of three parts: spirit, soul, and body. In other words, we are instructed to bring our body (flesh) into subjection to our recreated, regenerated, or "reborn" spirits.

I have lost weight supernaturally before. But now I am trying to lose weight by eating better. Sometimes I speak to my body and tell it to come into subjection to my spirit. I tell my stomach, "No, you are not going to have that donut; you are going to eat a salad and some water." Perhaps the Holy Spirit may convict you to unplug your cable television. One year I decided that I would not watch cable that year. I like to watch many programs on cable, but I don't love the commercials I see there because they pollute me. Certain programming pollutes my spirit man. Why should I to endure that and allow my eye gates and heart to become defiled?

Maybe you need to press into the Kingdom violently by turning your cable off. Or maybe you need to do a Facebook, Twitter, or Internet fast. If you do this, you will be bringing your body into subjection to your regenerated spirit. When you speak to your body and tell it to come into subjection to your regenerated spirit, guess what happens? Then you start to be led more so by your recreated spirit than led by your soul; your body recognizes your renewed spirit's authority and it obeys.

These are very practical and useful dynamics and keys we are learning about understanding the seer anointing, but they are very true precepts. Invest the time that you normally watch television and read about the seer experiences in the Scripture for one year. I guarantee that you will have a supernatural breakthrough into the seer anointing. Another key to activating your seer anointing is to pray in the Holy Spirit according to Jude 20. Pray in tongues for at least one hour per day. Praying in tongues can literally change your life and launch you into seer experiences!

Paul tells us in Ephesians 4:23 that is our responsibility to have our minds renewed or the spirit of our minds renewed. This deals with the transformation of our soulish or carnal nature; it deals with our worldly mindsets. An example of this type of worldly mindset was demonstrated to us by a wonderful man and woman we met at a conference. We sat down to dinner with them one evening and the man pulled out all these packages of foods and started eating from them. The conference provided a really good steak. So I'm enjoying my steak and this guy is eating things that are like hydrated or whatever. God wants us to enjoy life and eat good and healthy things!

I asked him, "Excuse me, don't you like steak?"

He answered, "Well, I've got gluten intolerance."

I responded, "Well, maybe you will get healed of that while you're here."

He responded back, "Oh, no. I don't want to be healed. I feel better. The doctor says if I eat this, that and the other thing I'll be OK; so I really like to eat this way."

I asked, "So you really like having gluten intolerance?"

He said, "Yes."

I shot back, "Well, what if God healed you?" He had a stronghold in his mind that convinced him he didn't want to be healed. It was a stronghold because of what the doctors had told him. We need to break those strongholds in our minds. Of course, God does give us a free will, and we can have anything that we desire, including gluten intolerance.

Part of what the monthly Jewish holiday Rosh Chodesh is all about is celebrating God's goodness and provision by eating good things. As we read in Genesis 1, God gave us the animals, the grains, and everything that bears fruit for food. He sanctified it and said it's for us to enjoy. I believe that we should enjoy life in fullness, yet in moderation. Hence, we bring our flesh into subjection to our spirit and eat "living" food and a healthy diet. This is very important to activating the seer anointing in your life because what we eat affects the purity of our body. When we eat unclean foods, we inhibit the Spirit of God from flowing efficiently through us, which enables us to see clearly and easily into the spiritual realm. A poor or unhealthy diet can hinder the seer anointing from activating fully in our lives.

Prayer for Healing

In the name of Jesus, I pray for total healing of gluten intolerance right now in Jesus' name. (Please feel free to insert any other sickness or condition that you are battling by name here.) I speak to that demon that causes people not to be able to process food correctly. And in the name of Jesus, I loose these people. I command food allergies to go in Jesus' name. I take authority over strongholds, word decrees, and curses spoken by health care professionals; and I command them to come to no effect. I speak the Kingdom of God over these. I thank You, Jesus, that You said we would prosper and be in health. Father,

*in the name of Jesus, I speak to those battling food allergies.
You told us Your kingdom come, Your will be done on earth
as it is in heaven. Lord, I thank You that in heaven we will
eat good things. You will withhold no good thing from those
who seek You. Father, I speak to pancreases, livers, stomachs,
esophagi, and whole digestive tracts; and in the name of Jesus,
I command them to line up with the Kingdom of God. Food
allergies must go now, in Jesus' mighty name. Lord, I ask in the
name of Jesus that You renew our minds and give us a Christ-
like mind today. Thank You, Lord. In Jesus I pray, Amen.*

You Have a Role to Play

Paul's teachings are referring to the sanctifying of our soul and the
reformation of our flesh. Only as we mature and begin to bring our
soul and flesh into submission to our spirit can we begin to enter
and entertain the spiritual aspects of Christ's Kingdom in fullness.
Some folks call this dynamic sanctification or walking in holiness.

It is important to understand that we have a part to play in this
process of sanctification. We need to renew our minds according
to the admonitions of Paul. Look at Romans 12:1-2: *"I beseech you
therefore, brethren, by the mercies of God, that you present your bodies a living sacrifice, holy, acceptable to God, which is your reasonable
service. And do not be conformed to this world, but be transformed by
the renewing of your mind, that you may prove what is that good and
acceptable and perfect will of God."*

These are keys that help unlock the seer anointing in our lives.
Now, let's continue to discover more scriptural principles that can
help us with this supernatural process of sanctification and the
renewing of our minds.

CHAPTER 6

Renewing and
Transforming Your Mind

Remember, Paul understood our triune nature because he learned it supernaturally as he was having revelatory experiences in the heavenly realms. Paul was a seer. He saw Jesus. Jesus appeared to him and spoke to him both in the heavenly realms and the natural realms. This is illustrated clearly in 2 Corinthians 12:2: *"I know a man in Christ who fourteen years ago—whether in the body I do not know, or whether out of the body I do not know, God knows—such a one was caught up to the third heaven."*

In Romans 12:1 Paul says, *"I beseech you therefore, brethren, by the mercies of God, that you present your bodies a living sacrifice, holy, acceptable to God, which is your reasonable service."* He is talking about bringing your flesh into subjection to your regenerated spirit. That is your reasonable service. If you want to be used by God and step into the seer anointing to recreate Christ in your sphere of influence, you will need to bring your body into subjection to your spirit and present it as an acceptable sacrifice to God. That can be one of your first fruits.

Sometimes God has a destiny for you but the enemy tries to hamper it with generational curses—it's in your bloodline. You may be battling generational curses that your father's, father's, father's father was involved in, so the devil thinks he has a right to oppress you. You can't seem to get free from that poverty, or you can't seem to get set free from those unclean lustful thoughts, or you can't seem to get set free from pornography, or whatever. If you are doing all the right things and you can't seem to get set free, maybe it's because it's demonic; it's a generational curse. You can get that yoke of darkness broken off of you.

I was under a curse of poverty. I'm not rich; I give more money away than I keep. But I was so poor that I could only afford to eat ramen noodles and Kool-Aid when I was in that little house when I first got saved. So I decided I was going to fast and pray and seek the Lord. And God has totally transformed my life. When it first started, I couldn't afford to give money to ministries but I could afford to pray for them. Then God began to give me a little bit of money and I began to give all of it away.

My family came to me and told me, "Kevin, you can't do what you're doing. You're too out there giving money to the poor. You can't go to Africa with all your money to preach and help orphans. You need to start saving some money for retirement." That is a stronghold. That's what the world says. In my opinion, that was an ungodly mindset. The word of God says, "*It is more blessed to give than to receive*" (Acts 20:35). In fact, the more money I give to the poor, the more money that God gives back to me. God gives seed to the sower (Isaiah 55:10; Luke 6:38). *Extravagant giving is another key to unlocking the hidden mysteries of the seer anointing in your life.*

Paul goes on in Romans 12:2, "*And do not be conformed to this world, but be transformed by the renewing of your mind, that you may prove what is that good and acceptable and perfect will of God.*" What's the perfect will of God? To have our mind's transformed. Does God say He's going to do it? No. He tells you to do it. By reading books and going to meetings that teach the truth, you are transforming your mind. As you get your mind transformed (your mind is part of your soul), your soul and then your flesh come into subjection to your recreated spirit. Then your recreated spirit becomes dominant in terms of your perception. And then God begins to open up your spiritual eyes and you can smell angels. God begins to open up your spiritual eyes and you can taste His Kingdom, you can taste and see that the Lord is good (see Psalm 34:8).

Did you know that you can see with your ears? Close your eyes and say, "Roses." What do you see? Did you see flowers? You didn't see with your eyes; you "saw" it with your ears. You can "see" with your five temporal senses.

Paul instructs us that it is also our reasonable service to have our minds renewed. We are also instructed to bring our flesh into submission to God in holiness. If you want to step into the seer realm, holiness is not an option. Am I perfect? Absolutely not! But, am I allowing the Holy Spirit to do a sanctification work in my body? You better believe it. You can too! Again, these are keys to help you step into the seer realm.

We must overcome unrighteous judgments and step into the glory and our lives will be transformed (John 7:24). This part is up to us. God does not promise to do that for us in His word. Unfortunately, very few people actually attempt or realize the need for sanctification. They look at that as something that was taught by the holiness preachers of the '40s and '50s. Many people today believe that we don't need holiness because it is not for today. It's in the word of God. You'd better believe you need it! Fewer still seek to implement the process of restoration, sanctification, and the renewing of their minds, which is an element of the soul. We can help activate the process of renewing our minds by washing our minds, will, and emotions with the power and anointing of God's word (see Ephesians 5:26).

The word of God is very important. Scripture washes and renews your mind. Read it daily. You need the word of God to renew your mind. Do you want to press into the Kingdom of God with violence? Get into the Scriptures. You can get the spoken Bible and play it at night when you are sleeping. Let the Scriptures repeat over and over and over again until God's word matriculates from your ears into your mind and settles into your spirit.

So as we study God's word and meditate upon God's word, our mind (which is the driving force of our soul) will be renewed and transformed into a Christ-like nature. Our soul (mind, will, and, emotions) will become Christ-like and we will learn how to be led by the Holy Spirit, not just for the moment but constantly. We will grow into the very nature and character of Jesus. Luxuriating in and upon the Scriptures everyday is a very important and practical way to activate the seer anointing in your life. The more that you meditate upon the Scriptures, the greater the level of the seer anointing that will manifest in your life.

When we learn to be led by the Spirit of God, we need to realize that it is a supernatural process. We must not get disappointed. It *is* a process. It's OK to make mistakes; it's OK if it doesn't happen instantaneously. Just keep pressing into the Kingdom of God. As this supernatural process begins to unfold in our lives, we will mature in Christ and initiate our transformation into His image and character. Once this happens we will be able to minister in the anointing of Jesus. We see this anointing, which is an elevated level of the seer anointing, found in Hebrews 4:14.

A Royal Priesthood

We have a great High Priest who has passed through the heavens, Jesus the Son of God, let us hold fast our confession (Hebrews 4:14).

We begin to understand that we, too, can pass through the heavens to seek revelation, authority, and power from the throne of God and enter into the very presence of God just like Christ. If the Lord opens up our spiritual eyes so we can see, what's that going to look like? We will be transformed into the nature of Christ and we are going to see the way Jesus saw. Jesus was a seer. In John 5:19 Jesus said He only does those things He sees His Father doing.

Remember the story of the woman caught in adultery in John 8? In verse 8 it tells how Jesus stooped down and wrote in the sand. There were many people standing around wanting to stone this woman to death, and Jesus is just looking down at the sand writing in it. Ever wonder what He was writing? I think it may have been the names and the dates of those who had been with her; it is possible that she was a prostitute. How did He know that? Maybe He "saw." God's a merciful God. He forgives us. Jesus was a seer. Though He sees our sins, He still loves us and died for us. That is amazing grace! God always see the potential and the gold in each of us.

When we grow in Christ-likeness, we will recreate Christ in our sphere of influence and become a priest forever according to the order of Melchizedek (see Hebrews 7:17). We will have the ability to recognize aspects from the spiritual realm. And as the Lord allows and gives us grace, we will actually demonstrate the ability to pass through the heavens, stepping *through* the temporal or earthly realm and entering *into* the spiritual realm. It's not so much going *up* into heaven, although we can. The heavenly realms are all around you at this instant. We only need to discern and *"see"* this fact.

The other day I went into the spiritual realm and I went to France, to Korea, to Malaysia, to Sierra Leone, to Brazil, and several other nations. I believe that as a direct result of this "seer experience," the door to South Korea opened to me. In this seer vision I stepped into the entrance of several jet bridges of airplanes. When I came back from that seer experience, I said, "Lord, what was that?" The Lord said, "Kevin, those are the eleven nations you are going to go to." I wrote them all down. We got invited to one of them almost immediately. The things in the spiritual realm are much more real than the things in the natural realm, and that's how the seer anointing works. We just do those things that we see our Father doing!

In fact, I just returned from South Korea where we saw the Lord release over sixty dental miracles where people had gold crowns supernaturally appear on their teeth! God did many other miracles and signs and wonders, with many saved and healed. Also, by the grace of God, three of my books were translated into the Korean language. The power of God released as we ministered in South Korea was tremendous. I believe that one reason for this outpouring was what I "saw" in the seer realm. I also believe that is what Jesus did. The Lord saw in the spiritual realm, and then He just did those things He saw on earth and miracles happened. I also believe that you can live a supernatural lifestyle of miracles, signs, and wonders like this too.

The Mantle of Melchizedek

It says in Hebrews 4:14 that we can pass through the heavens just like Jesus, the Son of God, did if we hold fast to our confession. But going into heaven and stepping into the heavenly realms is not always going *up* into heaven; sometimes it's about stepping *into* the spiritual realm that's all around us. When we can pass through the heavens or step into the spirit and seek revelation, authority, and power from the very throne of God, it can release us into our God-ordained destinies. In other words, we'll begin to minister in the anointing or mantle of Melchizedek. That just means that we are transformed into Christ-like character.

The mantle of Melchizedek is operating in the seer anointing and learning to live, breathe, and walk in the anointing of the Holy Spirit twenty-four hours a day, seven days a week, three hundred and sixty-five days a year. When we live in the realm of the seer anointing, we'll become mature seers. We'll be that golden eagle I wrote about earlier in the introduction of this book. We'll begin to soar into the heavenly realms, and then we will begin to speak and decree those things we see and hear. We'll become mature prophetic individuals; we'll become priests and prophets according to the order of Melchizedek.

The bottom line is that we will be mature sons and daughters of God, no longer tempered or tethered to the carnal realm by the weight of sin. When we walk in holiness, which is our reasonable sacrifice, we begin to free our spirit to step into or ascend to spiritual realms so that we can see, hear, smell, taste, touch, and discern those things that are more real than the book you are holding in your hands right now. When we see those things and begin to decree those things over our lives, we'll begin to see supernatural things happening—things like angels of prosperity coming to our house.

In the third of my trilogy of books, *Angels in the Realms of Heaven*, I tell about a time when I had been visiting heaven regularly and I went into the throne room of God. The angels and the great cloud of witnesses were singing in unison and the worship in the throne room was incredible. The glory of God was everywhere. I was walking with Jesus up to the throne. I thought, *This is not good because I know I have sin and I might not make it back out of here.* The closer we got to the throne, the more intense the glory became. The throne room is immense.

We walked for several miles through millions and millions of people. We came to twelve steps. I walked up those twelve steps. When I got up to the top, the Lord motioned to me and I stood beside Jesus. I watched as hundreds of people came and stood at the throne of God; they came and stood at the judgment seat of God. These people came and stood before Father God. Jesus came and stood beside many of them and was their advocate. Others stood at the judgment seat alone with no advocate. When I saw the lost standing at the judgment seat alone, it made me very sad and greatly and troubled my spirit. If you have the blood of Jesus covering you, He's your advocate (see Hebrews 12:22-29).

One day we will all stand before the judgment seat of God. The Lord will judge His people. I can tell you from personal experience, "it is a fearful thing to fall into the hands of the living God" (Hebrews 10:31). However, we need to understand that the judgment seat of God is a place of mercy and grace when Christ is your Savior. If you have never received Jesus Christ as your Lord and Savior, you can pray the prayer of salvation found at the end of this book right now.

In the next chapter we will look at several more scriptural principles that can help us to be transformed into mature sons and daughters of God and live in the seer anointing.

CHAPTER 7

Learning to Be Led by God's Spirit

It is possible for each of us to mature and to "grow up" into the very nature and character of Jesus Christ. As we submit to this process, we will begin to see our nature transformed. Our three-part or tri-une nature will begin to be turned inside out. Instead of being ruled and led by our soul and our flesh, we can be changed in a moment and in the twinkle of an eye. We will begin to see that we will be led by our "real self"—our spirit man.

Do you know what an earmark of being a son or daughter of God is? Romans 8:14 tell us it is those who are led by the Spirit of God: *"For as many as are led by the Spirit of God, these are sons of God."* Paul was talking about mature believers who have exercised their spiritual senses by reason of use, who have brought their soul— their minds, will, and emotions—into submission, and have had their minds sanctified by the washing of the word. They've become mature believers. They've begun to operate in a higher level of the giftings of the Holy Spirit, one of which is the seer anointing, a grace gift of the Spirit.

Paul understood this, and he teaches us that as children of God our spirits can become dominant for segments of time. Our spirit can become dominate, in terms of perception, for a few seconds, for a few minutes, or even a few days. That is what I believe happened to me during the season that I experienced the visitations into the heavenly realms which are documented in this book. It was during that season when my life was transformed. I believe that there is a grace for you to soar and to roar into the heavenly realms as well.

When I had the supernatural experience in 2002 at the Talapia Hotel in Mwanza, Tanzania, the Lord gave me specific instructions. Jesus told me that He was going to teach me about the seer anointing. Jesus also instructed me that in the future the day would come when He would release me to teach about the seer anointing to others. The Lord also instructed me to be diligent to search the Scriptures to learn more about the seer anointing.

He told me to start by looking at 1 Samuel 9:9: *"Formerly in Israel, when a man went to inquire of God, he spoke thus: 'Come, let us go to the seer'; for he who is now called a prophet was formerly called a seer."* When I read this scripture a little later, I was shocked because I did not realize that the word *seer* was actually in the Bible! I began the process of searching out the seers in the canon of Scripture. I want to encourage you to consider a similar study of the canon of Scripture if you are serious about activating the seer anointing in your life.

Later, in 2007, the ministry had been launched for three years. We were based in Kansas City at that time. One afternoon I was in prayer when suddenly I was taken up into heaven in a seer experience. I came to rest at a beautiful vista, and I was invited to sit beside Jesus on an immense precipice on a stone bench. The Lord pointed and said, "Look." I could see for miles and miles and miles. The Lord asked me again, "Do you see?"

I responded, "Lord, I'm sorry; I don't see."

He said, "Look again." When I did, it was like my ability to see multiplied; it was like I was looking at those mountains through a telescope. I could see them in great detail. Then Jesus said, "Look again." This time when I did, I could see even more clearly. The Lord asked me again, "Do you see?"

I responded again, "Lord, I'm sorry; I don't see."

He said, "Look a little higher."

And when I looked a little higher, I saw this immense eagle's nest with a lot of eggs in it. As I looked I saw the eggs begin to wobble and then little golden eaglets began to hatch out of the eggs. I saw a large mature golden eagle soar down and land upon the nest and nuzzle the eaglets. It was an immense golden eagle's nest. The Lord began to multiply my ability to see so I could see hundreds and hundreds of miles. I could see the large golden eagles well. I could even see the pupils of the mature golden eagle's eyes. Jesus pointed and I looked again, and I began to see little golden eaglets as they used their little egg tooth and came out of their eggs in this colossal golden eagle's nest. Jesus said, "Listen." I heard them begin to chirp. I began to hear them say, "Seers, seers, seers." The seer anointing involves both seeing and hearing well.

As I was sitting there on the granite bench in heaven, I saw the mature golden eagle take off and shriek. When the eagle shrieked, I was launched through time and space. I went from heaven to Africa. I went from 2007 to 2002. I was launched in the spirit back into the 2002 experience when I was in Mwanza. It seemed that I soared backwards in time. I was once again on the Sea of Glass Like Crystal and Jesus was once again standing over me. I relived that same experience where He taught me about the seer anointing for many hours.

I was once more lying on the shore of the Sea of Glass Like Crystal. That's when Jesus came; and I saw hundreds of angels ascending and descending upon Jesus. In the natural this took about three and one-half to four hours, but in the spirit it was a lot longer. This was when Jesus first began to teach me about the seer anointing. That's when I said, "Lord, I don't know about the seer anointing," and He said, "Begin to study it." So, I was excited to be hearing Jesus teaching me once more about the eminent release of His seers, because many times I have wished I had paid more attention or made better notes. However, I didn't know any better back then. (Here's a key: when God begins to activate the seer anointing in your life, write down the things that you see and hear in your seer experiences.) Let me encourage you to get into the habit of journaling all of your seer encounters. This is another key to exercising the seer anointing in your life.

That's why I have been able to share these stories with you; I write them down. So I am back in Mwanza seeing hundreds of God's angels ascending and descending upon Jesus. (The full testimony of this event is depicted in my book *Dancing With Angels 1*.) I listened to Jesus teach me about the seer anointing for a second time, and all of a sudden I hear an eagle screech and I am translated forward in time and I'm back in heaven on the granite bench. I think, *Wait a minute. Am I in Africa, am I in heaven, or am I in Kansas City?* Perhaps I was in all three places at the same time. This kind of bending of the time and space continuum is possible in the seer realm when the glory of God is hovering and moving in a place or upon an individual's life. Perhaps the glory and open heaven that rests upon Jesus initiated these seer experiences in Mwanza in 2002 and in Kansas City in 2007.

As this seer encounter unfolded in the heavenly realms in 2007, I was overcome by the glory and goodness of the Lord. Jesus looked deeply into my eyes as He stood up, and I knew it was time for me to stand up because this visitation into the realms of heaven was coming to an end. Jesus put His hands upon my shoulders and He said, "The time has come for you to begin to teach My people about the seer anointing." I shared before about how I had an encounter with a golden eagle and a lion—the lion roared at me and then the eagle shrieked at me on Tuesday, August 28, 2012, at 7:38 a.m. At that time the Lord stood behind me and tapped me on the shoulder. He said, "Go and tell My people that the time has come to roar and soar."

I believe we are at a kairos moment of time where anyone can step into this aspect of the Lord's Kingdom. God is raising up multitudes of seer prophets just like I saw multitudes of golden eagle eggs hatching in the heavenly realms. The Lord will raise up anointed eagles' nests that will train and equip these seers at this hour. We believe that the new King of Glory Ministries International Ministry Equipping Center (iMEC) in Moravian Falls, North Carolina, is one such eagle's nest. We hope to raise up a royal priesthood according to the order of Melchizedek. That simply means we will help people to become transformed into the very image of Jesus Christ, who is *the* Seer.

We have stepped into that kairos moment and season. The Lord is activating seers throughout the earth. The Lord will raise up ordinary people who will begin to be endued and anointed with the seer gift. This will actually be a restoration of the gift of discerning of spirits. Many regular people will begin to have the ability to see into the spirit and at times be released to co-labor with God's angels who are already busily working around each of us. Through understanding and operating in the seer anointing as mature sons and daughters of God, they will help win the great last days harvest for the glory of the King.

Harmony with the Holy Spirit

This will be the fruit of intimacy and understanding how to work in harmony with the Holy Spirit. And that's why I've written this book. You are a seer and there is going to be a grace for you to receive it. You can activate and experience the seer anointing. You can help initiate the process and assist the Holy Spirit to train your spirit to become dominate in terms of your perception. You are created to be a seer, and you can work with the Spirit of God to activate the seer anointing in your life.

When this process of our spirit becoming dominant begins to accelerate in our lives, we will begin to perceive attributes from the spiritual realm much more clearly than we did when we were driven by our carnal mind, intellect, soul, and flesh in terms of our perception. We will begin to perceive the spiritual realm in a much greater way, and the eyes of our spiritual understanding will be enlightened or opened to see, hear, taste, touch, and enter into the Kingdom of Heaven. This is the "seer anointing."

Of course, Jesus was our role model for this. I have outlined this aspect of Christ's mission and ministry on the earth in great detail in the book *The Sword of the Lord and the Rest of the Lord*. I encourage you to read this book. Also consider reading my trilogy of books, *The Reality of Angelic Ministry Today*, books 1, 2, and 3. These books are full of seer experiences. Read them more than one time as a way of exercising your spiritual senses by reason of use (Hebrews 5:14).

More importantly, I encourage you to begin to search the Scriptures looking for seer experiences. Read these passages in the Bible that were written by seer prophets. Read Ezekiel, John's Book of Revelation, and the Book of Daniel. Read Zechariah 5:1 where the seer prophet saw a flying scroll; "*Then I turned and raised my eyes, and saw there a flying scroll.*" Meditate on things like these, and ask yourself, "What did it look like to see a flying scroll?" This is a great exercise that can help activate your seer gifting. As of this writing I have been searching the Scriptures for more than a decade and continue to uncover new revelation from the word of God in reference to the seer anointing.

Enlightened Eyes of Understanding

We need to understand that Jesus shed His blood to make each of us kings and priests who would have the authority and the supernatural ability to have the eyes of our understanding be enlightened, to understand the hope of His calling for each of us, and to comprehend the riches of the glory of our inheritance. And also that we might know the exceeding greatness of His power toward each of us who believe through the working of His mighty power, which the Father worked in Christ when He raised Him from the dead and seated Him at His right hand in the heavenly places (see Ephesians 1:17-20). This is our calling and inheritance, and we can step into this supernatural calling in this lifetime. You can move in the seer anointing! You can pass through the heavens just like Jesus Christ modeled for us (Hebrews 4:14). You can step behind the veil that separates heaven and earth and grow into maturity as a seer.

The Creator of heaven and earth desires for each of us to have these same kinds of supernatural privileges as Jesus. The Lord Jesus blazed a trail and made a way for us to be seated at God's right hand in the heavenly places far above all principality, power, might, dominion, and every name that is named among men (see Ephesians 1:21). Jesus was our Forerunner in the seer anointing! Begin to get into the habit of asking the Lord to reveal to you the correlation between the glory realms and the seer anointing. Practice resting in the glory and tangible presence of God because resting in the glory can accelerate the activation of your seer gifting. This is another key to the seer anointing.

Be aware that there are seasons in our lives when we can be led more by our regenerated or reborn spirits than by our carnal and earthly mind, will, emotions, and our flesh. Embrace seasons like this. They are a precious kiss from heaven. It is during these times that the temporal realm will become secondary to us in terms of perception. We will begin to perceive more dominantly with our spirits and the eyes of our heart, or spiritual senses.

At these times we will begin to see and experience the reality of the spiritual Kingdom of God in a great and mighty way. Our spirits will perceive the reality of the spiritual realm in a dominate way. This dynamic is the spiritual gift of discerning of spirits that is activated in our lives. This is the manifestation of the seer anointing in a person's life. In the next chapter we will look at the seer anointing and the gift of discerning of spirits. This will help us uncover more spiritual principles which will help to activate the seer anointing in our lives.

CHAPTER 8

The Gift of Discerning of Spirits and the Seer Anointing

It is important that we understand how the Lord opens up our eyes to see into the spiritual realm. Let's begin to look at some scriptural principles that will help familiarize us with the process of how the Lord activates the seer anointing in our lives. Let's start by seeking to comprehend how it is possible for us to see into the spiritual realm or dimension. Some people call this ability to see into the spiritual realm "discernment." Discernment, which is the unction of the Holy Spirit, is not a *gift*; it is an *anointing* of the Holy Spirit. Some people say they have the "gift of discernment," but in my opinion there is no such thing. But there *is* a gift of discerning of spirits. There may be exceptions to every rule, and we will look at discernment in more detail later.

In 1 Corinthians 12, Paul lays out the gifts that the Holy Spirit gives to the Body of Christ. Verse 10 speaks specifically of the discerning of spirits: *"To another the working of miracles, to another prophecy, to another discerning of spirits."*

I find it interesting that the power gifts, as I call them—working of miracles and prophecy—are listed in conjunction with the gift of discerning of spirits. It's not a coincidence. If you read my other books, I talk about the chronological order of the restoration of the spiritual gifts to the Body of Christ. Starting with Azusa Street, all of the spiritual gifts have been restored to the Body of Christ *except* the gift of discerning of spirits. I believe we are at that moment in time when God is releasing and restoring the gift of discerning of spirits, which some people call the seer anointing, to His people. This gift of the Holy Spirit is actually the manifestation of the seer anointing in your life, although it's different. So sometimes in the Kingdom of God it can be both/and.

The ability to perceive spiritual things, such as angelic beings, is actually a gift given to ordinary people by the Holy Spirit. Let's look at the gifts of the Spirit (Holy Spirit), particularly this gift of discerning of spirits in more detail. As you begin to interact with the Kingdom of Heaven, you will experience many kinds supernatural encounters with Christ's Kingdom. As the seer anointing activates in your life, you may be given the grace to see into heavenly realms to interact with Christ, His Kingdom, God's angelic beings, and various places to be found there.

> *To another* [the Holy Spirit gives] *the working of miracles, to another prophecy, to another discerning of spirits, to another different kinds of tongues, to another the interpretation of tongues* (1 Corinthians 12:10).

You begin to see and hear things in the spiritual realm; you are becoming a mature son or daughter of God. You'll be able to step into the mantle of Melchizedek and, like Jesus, you'll only do those things you see and hear your Father doing.

Why did Jesus heal the blind sometimes by spitting in mud and rubbing it on their eyes and other times He just spoke a word? Why did Jesus lay hands on lepers sometimes and just speak a word at other times? Because He only did what He saw His Father doing. Jesus was a seer. If you want to do the greater works He's called you to, you need to step into the seer anointing too.

When the gift of discerning of spirits activates in your life, it is just one aspect of the seer anointing because the other spiritual gifts play a part in it; such as the word of wisdom or the word of knowledge. You can receive revelatory understanding from the seer realm in numerous ways, but it is all part of the seer anointing. Some of you may have a stronger gifting in a certain area that moves through you as the Holy Spirit wills. For example, some of you might smell spiritual things or taste spiritual things or hear spiritual things before you are able to see them.

The gift of discerning of spirits is crucial to the seer anointing; once it is activated, you will begin to see in the spirit. It is the Holy Spirit that gives to people the spiritual gift of discerning of spirits. The gift of discerning of spirits is a form of the seer anointing and surely is associated with the ability to see into the spiritual realm. Remember, when you have this gift of discerning of spirits activated in your life, you will begin to see things but it might not always be with your eyes. You can "see" more than one way.

I believe we are living in a kairos, God-ordained moment of time when whosoever will seek God with all of their heart will bring their flesh into submission to the regenerated spirit. They will have their mind renewed by the washing of the word. They will seek God with prayer and fasting. They will press into His Kingdom. They will seek teaching. They will seek impartation from God, first of all, and then from those people the Lord sends.

The gift of discerning of spirits is placed in Scripture among what are called the "power gifts" of miracles and healing. When we see into the spirit realm, sometimes we see demonic things. We are then able to take authority over them and break them off. Then we will see miracles and healing happen. That's part of the seer anointing— not just to be able to see the good stuff but also the ability to see the bad stuff and to understand that we have authority over those things because *"the weapons of our warfare are not carnal but mighty in God for pulling down strongholds"* (2 Corinthians 10:4).

Revisiting 1 Corinthians 12:10, it says, *"To another* [person is given] *the working of miracles, to another prophecy, to another discerning of spirits."* The word translated "spirits" in this passage of scripture is the Greek word *pneuma.*

Pneuma means, according to reference 4151 in Strong's Greek Concordance, a current of air, breath, the Spirit of God, the breath of God, Christ's Spirit, the Holy Spirit, a spirit, or an angel or demon. *Pneuma* is also the same word used for "spirits" in Hebrews 1:14.

> *But to which of the angels has He ever said: "Sit at My right hand, Till I make Your enemies Your footstool"? Are they not all ministering **spirits** sent forth to minister for those who will inherit salvation? (Hebrews 1:13-14, emphasis added).*

Remember that this scripture says angels are sent forth to minister "for," not "to." This gives this passage a whole new meaning. Most people assume that this scripture says "minister to" not "minister for." In the Amplified Bible, verse 14 is clarified: "*Are not angels all ministering spirits (servants) sent out in the service [of God for the assistance] of those who are to inherit salvation?*" God's angels are sent to serve you.

Clearly this Greek word *pneuma* can refer to angels. It is clear that the gift of discerning of spirits can refer to the ability or gift to comprehend or to see or to discern the presence of angelic beings or other attributes from the spirit. It can also refer to seeing and discerning demonic beings or other things in the spirit, such as the Holy Spirit or the presence of the glory or the fragrances of heaven like frankincense. These things come from the discerning of spirits being activated in your life. This gift is a lot more than just seeing angels; it is a lot more than just discernment; it is an aspect of what many call the "seer anointing."

The spiritual gift of discerning of spirits is the ability to discern or recognize beings (good or evil) from the spiritual realm. When your spiritual eyes are activated and you begin to operate in the gift of discerning of spirits, or the seer anointing, you will see both the angelic realm and the demonic realm. We will look at this dynamic of the seer anointing in more detail in the subsequent chapters.

The definition of the "gift of discerning of spirits" is the ability to discern or recognize supernatural beings (good or evil) from the spiritual realm. It is the God-given supernatural insight into the spirit world—literally being given (as the Holy Spirit wills) the ability to see, hear, comprehend, and understand information obtained in the realm of spirit.

This definition can also apply to the seer anointing, although the seer anointing is broader and farther reaching than the gift of discerning of spirits. We will discuss this in more detail later in the book. As you read this book, I believe there will be a grace and activation to release of the gift of discerning of spirits or the fullness of the seer anointing into your life.

Prayer of Activation

Father, I thank You for Your word. I pray that You would seal Your words in the spirits—hearts—of Your people. I ask that You would seal Your words in the soul—mind, will, and emotions—of Your people. I ask, Father God, that You would release Your word to minister to the Body of Christ. Lord, we give You the praise and the honor and the glory for Your word and for everything that You are about to do. Lord, we thank You for all the wonderful things You have already done.

I thank You that You are going to open up eyes, that You are going to give us eyes to see and ears to hear. Lord, I ask You in Jesus' name, that if we have hearts that are dull and ears that are heavy and eyes that are spiritually blind that You would open up our hearts, open up our ears, open up our eyes, and open up everything within us, God. Activate and bring it alive in us, Lord, so that we would have spiritual eyes to see and that we would have spiritual ears to hear. Lord, recreate our hearts according to Psalm 51; create in us clean hearts so that we can walk in holiness and the very image of Jesus and that we can step into the realms of Your Kingdom.

Lord, You tell us in Proverbs 25:2 that the hidden and mysterious things of Your Kingdom are put there for us to dig out; and we thank You for that. I thank You that the blood of

Jesus has made us kings and queens and priests and that You reveal Your hidden treasures to those who seek You.

Father, I remind You that Your word says in Luke 12:32 that it is Your good pleasure to give the Kingdom of God to those who are seeking You. So I pray for activation and release impartation.

Holy Spirit, come. I ask for the winds of heaven to come and touch hearts. Heal all the broken hearts. I ask that You would remove the hoods that have been placed over heads because of generational curses. I thank You, God, that You are setting us free. Thank You that You are removing yokes of darkness that have hindered our ability to see. Thank You, Lord, that we shall arise.

In the next chapter we will look at some amazing testimonies of God's faithfulness to release the seer anointing. We will also discover several more keys to help you activate your seer gifting and transform who you are in Christ.

CHAPTER 9

An Encouraging Testimony of Activation and Transformation

This is a brief testimony of how God opened up my spiritual eyes. The whole process was really quite simple and easy. I hope that by including this testimony you will be encouraged that God can release a similar activation of the seer anointing in your life too.

From the very beginning of my walk with Jesus, the supernatural aspects of the Lord have been evident in my life. God has done amazing things. There have been segments of time when He has opened up my eyes and allowed me to see into the spiritual realm. This was truly the grace and mercy of God. This began happening almost immediately after I was born again—born from the heavenly realms—when my spirit was reactivated and I came back into the family of God. Although at that time I'd never heard the word *seer* and didn't know what it meant, I began to experience and walk in the dynamics of the seer anointing. Why? Because this realm is available to whosoever today. I believe that one reason for this shift is that there is an acceleration of the ingathering of the great last days harvest (Matthew 9:36-38; Luke 10:2).

When you are outside the ark of safety (Christ's salvation), when you are a child of darkness, you can't hear God's voice very clearly. However, at times God does speak to us or nudge us through the work and ministry of the Holy Spirit; otherwise we wouldn't be saved.

God began to communicate with me as a new believer in different ways and began to speak to me very clearly. First God spoke to me through the Scriptures. Then the Lord communicated powerfully to me through nature. I actually heard the audible voice of the Lord. I had a visitation where God began to speak to me. God sent angelic beings to me. These godly angels came into my brother's living room, and I began to hear the Lord speak to me and give me directives for evangelism in my home town. I was obedient to these instructions, even though I was not trained to work as an evangelist by the church (this lack of training caused difficulties with some local pastors, God bless them). However, I knew that I had heard from God and choose to be obedient to the supernatural instructions I was given in the seer realm.

Let me also state that it is very important to be in submission to spiritual authority. *Ask God to place you into submission to the spiritual authority **He** ordains for you.* This is very important. Obedience is one of the most important keys to unlocking and maintaining the seer anointing in your life.

Other manifestations of God's Kingdom came to my five temporal senses. When I would pick up my old King James Bible, I began to smell the fragrances of heaven (frankincense, calamus, and myrrh). These heavenly fragrances seemed to be emanating from the binding of that beat up old book! Because that is what I experienced, I thought that this kind of sign and wonder was supposed to happen every time that you read the Bible! I smelled the pungent fragrances of frankincense, calamus, myrrh, cinnamon, and roses almost every time I read the Scriptures for months. I now know that people call this the "fragrance of the Lord"; but as a new believer, I just thought this was normal Christianity.

Today it is not uncommon for people to smell the fragrances of heaven in our Gospel meetings. I still think it is just normal! This is one way that the seer anointing can manifest in your life—through your sense of smell. You can discern the heavenly realms by smelling the fragrances of heaven. Even as I am writing this paragraph I sense the fragrances of heaven wafting around me. I know by revelation that many of you reading this right now will have your *spiritual* sense of smell activated to smell the fragrances of heaven too! Hallelujah!

During this season I also began to sense or feel the heavy, weighty presence of the glory of God (Shekinah glory). God's Shekinah glory would pin me down on the old couch where I slept. I could actually taste supernatural fragrances from time to time. I began to feel physical sensations as the Kingdom of God began to manifest in my life and within my sphere of influence. Perhaps you may be experiencing the Shekinah glory of God falling upon you as you read this. If you do, just put this book down and go and find a comfortable spot and rest in the glory. This will help to accelerate the activation of the seer anointing in your life! Amen!

Soon I began to experience visions, or what some call third heaven encounters, as the Lord activated the gift of discerning of spirits in my life. I began to see and discern things from the spiritual realm. I thought all this was normal. It wasn't until about nine months later that I found out most Christians (mostly church leaders) considered these kinds of supernatural seer experiences to be weird or even creepy. I just embraced these supernatural experiences as natural for a born-again child of God. They were in the Bible, and I just assumed they were supposed to happen to Christians today. Even though these kinds of supernatural experiences were very biblical, many in the church rejected and scorned them. It bears repeating; you may need to forget some religious doctrines and overcome ungodly mindsets that you may have unwittingly been indoctrinated with in order to embrace the seer realm fully (Matthew 15:7-9; 18:3).

I am sharing these short testimonies to illustrate to you that the seer anointing is much more than simply seeing into the spiritual realm. As I saw these kinds of supernatural experiences in the Bible, I just embraced them! My wife, Kathy, and I embrace the Kingdom of God and its fullness in our lives. The truth is that every Christian *is* supposed to experience supernatural encounters with Christ and His Kingdom.

Because I have experienced supernatural encounters from the Lord and in His Kingdom from the very inception of my Christian walk, I did not question the mystical aspects of the Kingdom of God. I had not been brought up in the church and had not been indoctrinated to believe that supernatural experiences were not intended to be a normal part of walking with Jesus today. You should not be *paranoid of the paranormal* aspects of our God because He is a supernatural Being.

Launched into His Presence

After I had been saved a short time, I had been praying and asking the Lord what He wanted me to do. I knew through the unction of the Holy Spirit that God had a destiny for me; in fact, I had been predestined (Romans 8:29). I knew that it wasn't to continue to do the sinful things I'd done in the past. I knew that I needed to be sanctified. Even though I didn't understand it or have any theology for it, I knew I needed to change. I just knew that God had a purpose for me. I noticed in my old King James Bible that Jesus fasted and prayed, so I began to fast and pray and ask the Lord about this. The Creator of the heavens and the earth surely has a destiny for you too.

In my previous books I wrote about an early vision when I saw Jesus clearly in the spirit. He was waving at me and calling me to draw closer to Him. Jesus was holding out His arms inviting and welcoming me to come into His presence. I had a decision to make. Either I would go to Jesus or I would dismiss this vision (seer realm) and continue to pray to Him in my little prayer closet. In my heart I made a decision to go to Him: "Yes, Lord, I'll come." Immediately I had a sense of being catapulted through time and space. A minute later I found myself in the very presence of Jesus Christ. I fell down at His feet and began to weep because I truly felt the love of God for the first time in my life. *Let me encourage not to dismiss seer experiences too quickly, as they can begin very subtlety. You need to learn to develop sensitivity to the Spirit of God.*

God has such a consuming and amazing love for every single one of us. Our human minds cannot comprehend the width and length and depth and height of the love of God for every tribe, every tongue, every nation (Ephesians 3:18-19). As Jesus wrapped His arms around me, I was overcome by the billows and billows and billows of His powerful love that washed over me. I began to weep and weep and weep. After some time had passed the Lord hugged me tightly, and it felt as if I was being washed and thoroughly cleansed by His pure love and all encompassing compassion. Later, Jesus gently moved me away from His chest and looked deeply into my eyes and He said, "Kevin, I have called you here today to tell you who you are."

My destiny was being birthed, and your destiny can be activated too. It is not too late for you. I was forty-two years old. I had wasted thirty years of my life in drug and alcohol addiction. God has restored everything that I lost. God has accelerated my life and given me the privilege to travel to thirty-three nations to share the Gospel of the Kingdom. How did that happen? I stepped into the heavenly realms. The seer anointing activated in my life. When we step into the spiritual realm and God begins to give us supernatural revelation from there, it can move the mountains in our life immediately (Mark 11:22). When we begin to see and hear from the spiritual realm, our life becomes transformed. That's what God did for me. He transformed my life in a supernatural way. The seer realm can initiate a supernatural and God-ordained exchange in your life too.

As I was being held by Jesus and washed in the purity of His unfathomable love, I cried uncontrollably. I was receiving deliverance and cleansing. As He stepped back from me, the Lord said, "Kevin, today I'm going to tell you who you are. I've called you to be an artist, an author, and an evangelist." This was the answer to my prayers and fasting. Those words penetrated to the very depth and fiber of my being.

When I stepped back from the Lord, I saw that He was flanked by four strong angels. These enchanting creatures seemed to be overjoyed that I was there in the presence of Jesus. The angels welcomed me as they smiled at me with assurance. Jesus moved His right hand in a sweeping motion indicating the four angels that were present. He said; "Today I am appointing these angels to your ministry." This statement baffled me. I thought, *Wait a minute, I just got saved, I have no money, I haven't been to Bible college—what do You mean, ministry?* It just blew my mind.

It seems to me that Jesus looks at things a little differently than many of us do in the church. Perhaps, we are a little arrogant about what we "think we know" (our doctrine) about the Lord Jesus and His Kingdom. Perhaps, we are a little too comfortable with our miniscule and petty understanding of the Creator of the heavens and the earth and His grace.

Stepping Into the Seer Anointing

In my carnal way of thinking, Jesus' words made no sense. But in the Kingdom of God and the spiritual realm, I had a destiny, just as you have a destiny. Your destiny is to recreate Christ in your sphere of influence. One of the ways you can do that is by pressing into the Kingdom of God and activating your ability to see and hear from the heavenly or spiritual realms like I have shared in the previous testimony. Be diligent to get the seer anointing activated in your life. You are a seer. I believe that we have entered into a God-ordained moment of time when the Lord is releasing multitudes of people to step into the realm of the seer anointing.

Just as quickly as it began, this seer vision and experience was over. However, the feeling of Christ's supernatural love and presence rested upon me for days after that amazing supernatural encounter. When the vision ended I found myself back in my prayer closet weeping. For several months I wept every time this event came into my mind. This vision helped launched me deeper into the seer realm. I pray that as you read this testimony that Elohim will launch you deeper into the seer realm as well.

Many people walk in a remarkable level of supernatural activity today. Throughout the Bible there are accounts of many people living in a very high level of the seer realm. Of course, Jesus Christ is our role model for this kind of seer lifestyle. As more and more people begin to operate in the seer anointing in their everyday lives, miracles, signs, wonders, and even angelic encounters will become more common today. These kinds of supernatural experiences and outpourings of the Holy Spirit did not stop at the Book of Acts.

When the Lord spoke to me in Africa and told me I needed to learn about the seer anointing, I said, "Lord, I never heard that. What is that?" He told me to study the Book of 1 Samuel about the seers. I don't claim to have the full revelation on the seer anointing, but the Lord has shown me a few more things that I want to share with you in the subsequent chapters.

As you hear or read testimonies of people who have had seer experiences, such as going to heaven, I believe this will increase your faith. The Kingdom of God is within you and the Kingdom of God is real. God wants you to taste and see and hear the Kingdom of God. More than that, He wants you to inherit the Kingdom of God—not just when you die, but in this life. That is what the seer anointing is all about.

I believe that you can have experiences like the ones described in this chapter. Perhaps there is a grace upon my life to release an impartation of the seer anointing through books like this one. It is not necessary for me to lay hands on you to release activation or an impartation. I was not a theologian, nor am I one now, nor do I wish to become one. I am a full-grown man who is seeking to grow up to become a little child; a child of my heavenly Father. I was not an elder of the church. In fact, I was a novice! I had not even read the whole New Testament when the God of the universe invaded my time and space. That is what I want you to grasp. Many churches and ministries instill an ungodly belief system into our hearts that insinuates that we can only grow closer to God as we serve a religious system.

I don't believe that God looks at His Kingdom that way. In fact, the blood of Jesus Christ makes you righteous and holy to serve and approach the Lord. There is nothing that you can "do" or learn in the church that will make you any more righteous or holy. We see this in Revelation 1:5-6: *"Jesus Christ, the faithful witness, the firstborn from the dead, and the ruler over the kings of the earth. To Him who loved us and washed us from our sins in His own blood, and has made us kings and priests to His God and Father, to Him be glory and dominion forever and ever. Amen."*

This is purely the grace of God. I call this apostolic love. (Look for the teaching CD or the MP3 download entitled *Apostolic Love*.) What I am seeking to say is that God is more than able to activate us into the gifts of the Spirit, like the seer anointing, and release us into amazing supernatural encounters outside of the church. However, I want to say that we love the church. But the "church" as we know it now is changing (Luke 5:37-38).

Don't get me wrong. We need the church, and it will never be replaced. But it will change from the way we understand it today. I am a member of a church. I am submitted to the pastor of a church. Kathy and I tithe to our home church faithfully. As we have traveled we have found that this is a widespread "feeling" within many believers' hearts today. Many people do not feel comfortable and sense that they do not "fit into" church. Let me suggest that what you are feeling may not be the devil, as some suggest. Perhaps the uncomfortable feeling you are discerning is the Lord. Perhaps the Holy Spirit is wooing you to invest some time in the Secret Place with Him outside of the four walls of the church.

It is likely that when God begins to activate the seer anointing in your life you may not be "well received" by the church. That is OK because God Himself can supernaturally establish you in your God-ordained destiny in His Kingdom. Having said all of that, I do wish to encourage you to submit to spiritual authority. There is much to say on this sensitive subject, and I encourage you to read my new book, *Unlocking the Mysteries of the Powers of the Age to Come*.

In that book I write about the new structure of the church as we move from the church age to the new apostolic age in the church. You see, at this hour the structure of the Body of Christ has already been transformed in the spiritual realm. This issue is that the earthly church structure is not ready to embrace this new move of God that is upon the horizon, but the church soon will! Perhaps you feel unable to find a church of ministry that you "feel at home" in. If that is the case, don't worry. I believe that the Spirit of the Lord is calling many people outside of the "traditional church structure." The Lord is seeking to set His friends aside and teach them One on one, Spirit to spirit, and to speak to us, and teach us as a man does to a friend (John 15:15).

Just pray this prayer of activation now. Pray it out loud, and feel free to pray it frequently as the Holy Spirit leads you.

Prayer of Transformation

Father, thank You for the glory and thank You for the heavens that are open and the free access You have given us to the heavenly realms. Lord, I thank You for ears to hear and eyes to see. Father, I thank You that You are massaging our hearts, making them tender towards Your word. I prophesy and decree, Father God, that Your word will not return void but it will accomplish everything that You have set for it to do. We give You the praise and the honor and the glory for all that You do. Thank You, Lord, for opening my spiritual eyes to see and my spiritual ears to hear and discern.

In the next chapter we will discover why this is *"the time"* for your spiritual eyes to be opened and for the seer anointing to activate in your life.

CHAPTER 10

A Kairos Moment of Time

We are moving from the church age to the new apostolic age in the Body of Christ. As a result the Lord is dealing with His people differently today. God has brought you upon the planet Earth *"for such a time as this"* (Esther 4:14). I believe that we are living in a day and an hour that some of the great cloud of witnesses long to see (Hebrews 12:1). The following scripture perfectly describes the day and hour in which we now live: *"Eye has not seen, nor ear heard, Nor have entered into the heart of man The things which God has prepared for those who love Him"* (1 Corinthians 2:9).

In writing to the Corinthian church, Paul put his own expression on what had been written by Isaiah so many years before in Isaiah 64:4. My expression of this same concept reads this way: Our eyes have not seen, nor our ears heard, nor has it dawned upon our hearts the extraordinary things which God has prepared for those who love Him. The Lord wants for you to see some amazing supernatural things!

What did we learn from the Book of John about those who love God? *"He who loves Me will be loved by My Father, and I will love him and manifest Myself to him"* (John 14:21). God promises He would "manifest" Himself; display Himself like a fine Renaissance painting on a wall. That means to visit or to show a thing plainly. That means that God will come and have tea with you. That means He will dance with you. These kinds of supernatural experiences most often occur during worship. This is an activation of the seer anointing. These

63

kinds of visitations of the Lord can happen while we are still on this side of eternity and still in this earth suit. Again, worshiping God consistently is a key to activating the seer anointing in your life.

God is looking for those He can anoint, endue, smear, activate, and release the seer anointing to. *Let me encourage you to just believe to receive God's anointing to see!*

Learn To Hear from the Lord Yourself

We need to listen to the Lord and His prophets. We need to have 20/20 vision like we see in 2 Chronicles 20:20: *"Jehoshaphat stood and said, 'Hear me, O Judah and you inhabitants of Jerusalem: Believe in the Lord your God, and you shall be established; believe His prophets, and you shall prosper.'"* That being said, there is an issue we find in the Body of Christ today of an unhealthy reliance on prophetic ministry. In some streams of the Body, the office of a prophet has been elevated to the point where it becomes idol worship.

We need to hear from the Lord for ourselves at this time. We need to know whether or not a word is from the Lord, no matter who says it. That is one reason it is so important to learn to step into the seer anointing—so we can hear, see, taste, smell, touch, and understand what God is doing in our sphere of influence and not depend on every digital prophetic word that comes down the electronic pike.

Scripture uses different words in the original language that are translated "prophet" and "seer." The bottom line is that the seer anointing is a different level of the prophet anointing, which is a type of charismatic or spiritual gift.

If God opens up your eyes so you begin to see, that doesn't mean you are any better than a word prophet or a *nabi* prophet (such as Nathan). It only means that your anointing is different. We are all one body and we must work together in unity. That's why David had both the seer and the *nabi* prophet advise him. God needs both. God still releases and uses both types of these two prophetic anointings today.

We see a scriptural example of this in 2 Chronicles 29:25: *"And he stationed the Levites in the house of the Lord with cymbals, with stringed instruments, and with harps, according to the commandment of David, of Gad the king's seer, and of Nathan the prophet; for thus was the commandment of the Lord by His prophets."* Seer prophets are often signs and wonders prophets. They have exercised their spiritual senses by reason of use (Hebrews 5:14). Many times miracles will accompany their preaching.

In this kairos moment of time, God is anointing whosoever. And as these "whosoevers" preach the Gospel, they will get revelatory knowledge. And as they do the things they see God doing, miraculous things will happen like in the life of Jesus. We have this promise from Jesus in John 14:12: *"Most assuredly, I say to you, he who believes in Me, the works that I do he will do also; and greater works than these he will do."*

Jesus is the *seer.* The disciples saw all the things He did and they also became seers themselves. This began at Jesus' baptism, when they saw the Holy Spirit descend in the bodily form of a dove and they heard the Father speak (Luke 3:22). It was strengthened at the Mount of Transfiguration, when they saw Moses and Elijah and they heard the Father speaking directly to them (Matthew 17:1-6). In Acts 2 they were endued with power, and in Acts 4 greater power came on them. It was at this point that they began to declare the word of God with boldness. Why was this? Because they had matured and could now see clearly into the spiritual realm. They began to hear the Spirit of God speaking to them very well (Acts 13:2). When they did those things they saw their Father doing, miracles happened.

In this day and hour in which we live, God wants to speak to you. God wants all of us to work miracles. The seer anointing is available to whosoever. There is not one instance in the New Testament where the gifts of God are delegated exclusively to a chosen vessel. This was not the case in the Old Testament, but it is always for *whosoever* in this dispensation of grace. I believe that any other belief is ungodly and needs to be washed from your mind. This is my opinion. God wants you to walk in power and signs and wonders. God wants you to display the glory of God so people will say, "What in the world is going on?" They will be drawn to the rising of the glory of Christ in you. Supernatural signs will make the lost in the world wonder.

God is looking for mature sons and daughters who will begin to prophesy according to the Spirit of God; mature sons and daughters who will be led by the Spirit of God. When these mighty ones (the army of God) speak and decree, demonstrations (miracles, signs, and wonders) of the Kingdom of Heaven will come. The eyes of the Lord are searching for ordinary people that He can use through whom He will release the seer anointing at this hour.

The Eyes of the Lord—
God Is Looking for Seers Like You

For the eyes of the Lord run to and fro throughout the whole earth, to show Himself strong on behalf of those whose heart is loyal to Him (2 Chronicles 16:9).

Remember, God is seer. God is looking for other seers through whom He can pour out His love and manifest Christ's Kingdom. God is looking for people that He can pour out His Spirit upon. How does He look? In this scripture the eyes of the Lord are angelic beings that run to and fro throughout the earth. These eyes of the Lord are looking for those who have a heart loyal to God. The eyes of the Lord are running to and fro throughout the earth looking for those who have clean hands and a pure heart.

The eyes of the Lord are running to and fro throughout the world seeking those who are sold out for God, who are walking in holiness, who have a passion to recreate Christ in their life. The eyes of the Lord are running to and fro throughout the whole earth seeking those who God can show Himself strong on their behalf. God is seeking mature sons and daughters to endue with heavenly power and authority.

We are entering into a season or appointed time for us to lay down our personal agendas. It is imperative that we begin to demonstrate the Gospel of the Kingdom. An important aspect of this will be releasing or manifesting the Kingdom of God the same way

Jesus did. One of the many tools the Lord has given us to release His power and manifest His Kingdom is the seer anointing.

The Lord is doing glorious things in the earth today. The veil between the heavens and earth is thin, fragile, and more transparent than at any time in history. As the triumphant return of Christ approaches, the amount of supernatural activity of Elohim, the Creator of heaven and earth, will dramatically increase. This now includes a great increase in the seer anointing.

The messages that I am sharing in this book were birthed over the last decade. During this time I've sought the Lord diligently about supernatural encounters and seer experiences that I have lived through. I have come to a conclusion as I have fasted, prayed, and researched the Scriptures concerning the seer anointing: It has always been God's plan and intention to allow ordinary people to see, interact, experience, discern, and enter into His Kingdom.

The Lord has called everyone to be aware of His spiritual Kingdom. Anyone can experience the supernatural realm of the seer anointing. The seer anointing should be a normal part of your life too. However, I wanted to encourage you in this chapter that we have entered into a God-ordained time—a time when the God of the universe is actively seeking friends that He can endue with the seer anointing. Amen! In the next chapter we will look at several scriptural principles to help you achieve a closer walk with the Holy Spirit.

CHAPTER 11

The Unction of the Holy Spirit and the Seer Anointing

But ye have an unction from the Holy One, and ye know all things (1 John 2:20, KJV).

John the revelator wrote this. He was one of the three people Jesus took into a specific geographic place where the heavens were opened so that their spiritual senses could be activated (Luke 9:28-36; Matthew 17:1-13).

When we walk in intimacy, closeness, and communion with God, we begin to have an activation of our spiritual senses too. We will be given unction from the Holy One to activate and co-labor with the Holy Spirit to release tasks and to accomplish purposes for God's Kingdom on earth at this hour. The unction of the Holy Spirit is another aspect of the seer anointing. Some of these unctions might be, for instance, helping orphans half a world away or preaching the Gospel to the ends of the earth by Internet. Whatever God has called you do, the Holy One can give you revelatory knowledge how to obtain, release, and activate your destiny. Developing the unction of the Holy One in your life only comes by investing time in the presence of the Holy Spirit.

By the way, according to the Merriam-Webster Dictionary, the word *unction* is defined as "rubbing or sprinkling of oil on somebody as part of a religious ceremony or the act of anointing as a rite of consecration or healing, especially with regard to spiritual matters and especially when expressed in suitably solemn language." To have an unction of the Holy Spirit is to be anointed by the Holy Spirit for a specific task or purpose; like, for example, the seer anointing.

Did you know God the Father, God the Son, and God the Holy Spirit all have a different voice? And we can recognize each one. The Holy Spirit longs to speak to you. When "the Holy Spirit said" in Acts 13:2, that's what launched Paul into his international ministry. Before the Holy Spirit spoke to the believers in Antioch, Paul was just a reborn Pharisee, not an apostle. Hearing God's voice well is an important aspect of the seer anointing. And the unction of the Holy Spirit can be the catalyst that launches you into your God-ordained destiny too.

Here is some great news for you! Every one of you reading this now has something that Peter, James, or John didn't have when they started their ministry. You have the Holy Spirit inside of you; they did not have the Holy Spirit inside of them when they met Jesus. It was not until the Day of Pentecost that they received the Holy Spirit. Through the unction of the Holy Spirit that dwells inside of you, you can know all things. That is a level of the seer anointing. Some people mistakenly call it the gift of discernment. I have only met one man who has a gift of discernment. He developed his extraordinary anointing over four decades of ministry. I have never met another person who I feel actually has a "gift" of discernment. Perhaps there are exceptions to every perceived rule, though.

There is a gift of discerning of spirits which we looked at earlier. But what I'm talking about is an unction of the Holy Spirit where you can have revelatory knowledge, where you can be led by the Spirit without God necessarily speaking to you in a voice. You can have a witness in your spirit or an unction of the Holy Spirit that you are supposed to be in a certain place at a certain time. This is not the still small voice of the Holy Spirit. This is an operation or manifestation of the seer anointing. God wants you to learn to co-labor with His Spirit like this. It's life changing. It's real.

Each morning I bow my knees and pray the prayer from Ephesians 1:16-21 to build up my spirit to prepare for the things God has for me. God hears prayers like that because, as we discovered in the last chapter, *"The eyes of the Lord run to and fro throughout the whole earth, to show Himself strong on behalf of those whose heart is loyal to Him"* (2 Chronicles 16:9).

God will empower and equip ordinary people with the seer anointing. We will see into the spiritual realms and work in harmony with God's Spirit to impact our environment and our sphere of influence for God's glory. This will be pivotal to usher in the approaching global healing revivals and outpourings of God's Spirit that will soon cover the earth.

The Seer Anointing and Angelic Ministry

Jesus promises you and me authority for this kind of ministry, which is one aspect of the seer anointing. Let's look at this in Matthew 16:19: *"I will give you the keys of the kingdom of heaven, and whatever you bind on earth will be bound in heaven, and whatever you loose on earth will be loosed in heaven."*

At times the seer anointing and the unction of the Holy Spirit will allow us to see into the heavenly realms to work and co-labor with God's agents of revival there—angelic beings. However, we must remember that **Christ Jesus must be the absolute cornerstone of our faith.** Our faith must always be rooted and grounded in Jesus Christ. We must worship the Lord alone and seek His perfect plans for our lives. We are never to worship angels, as this is strictly forbidden in Scripture. (See Colossians 2:18 and Revelation 19:10.)

However, we need to realize that at this time in history God is releasing to us another arrow for our quiver of spiritual weapons of warfare—the grace to co-labor with God's angels. We can co-labor with God's angels when we are released by the unction of the Holy Spirit. As with other aspects of the seer anointing, learning to co-labor with angels is a learning curve. (Read my trilogy of books, *Dancing with Angels*, books 1, 2, or 3, or listen to the audio messages in the Dancing with Angels School of the Supernatural for more in-depth teaching on this subject.)

Angels are an important and essential part of God's Kingdom. Are they not ministering spirits sent forth to minister *for* those who will inherit salvation? (See Hebrews 1:14.) It's a lot different to have an angel minister *for* you rather than *to* you. When the Lord opens your eyes and activates your seer gifting, you will most likely begin to see angels. When you have the gift of discerning of spirits functioning in your life, you can understand how angels have come to minister *for* you. There is often angelic ministry involved when healing takes place.

It is quite possible that the Lord may be planning to use His angelic hosts to meet your needs in the coming days. As we enter into this new season, we must be open to God's perfect will. Remember, if the Lord allows you to see His angels, it is for a purpose.

"That Was Easy"

Seeing into the spirit is easy. It is an elementary part of the Kingdom of God. One time Jesus came to me with something in His hand; He held it out to me. It was an "easy" button.

I said, "Jesus, You've got an easy button."

He said, "That's right, and you can have it." And He handed it to me.

I said, "What am I supposed to do with this?"

He said, "Press it."

When I hit the button, the words "that was easy" sounded off! Then whoosh, I supernaturally ascended up into the heavens! So there Jesus was in the heavens to meet me! I said, "Lord, that was really amazing! What do you want me to do with this easy button?"

He said, "Tell My people they can *all* have an easy button. It's going to be easy to ascend into the realms of the heavens at this hour." That's the day and the hour that we live in. This, too, is an aspect of the seer anointing.

Jesus said, "*And I will give you the keys of the kingdom of heaven, and whatever you bind on earth will be bound in heaven, and whatever you loose on earth will be loosed in heaven*" (Matthew 16:19). At times when the seer anointing is activated in your life, you will be released to co-labor with things in the heavenly realm. At times the Lord may open up your eyes and give you the unction of the Holy Spirit to activate or loose an angel for a specific purpose. The Lord's angels are looking to see whom they can help. The unction of the Holy Spirit can activate us to loose God's angelic beings in the heavenly realms to impact circumstances upon the earth. This is yet another way that you can minister in the seer anointing.

Sometimes when God activates your spiritual senses, you can discern those kinds of supernatural things. In the third book of my trilogy, I tell of a diamond the size of a golf ball that Jesus gave me in the heavenly realms. There was a purpose for that diamond. There was supernatural revelation that came from that diamond. I believe that it was the revelation for the books. At other times the Lord will allow you to see or discern things other than objects like supernatural treasures. You can learn to discern or see demonic weapons and demonic beings. In the next chapter we will look at some scriptural keys and weapons to help you when you see demonic things in the second heaven or temporal realm.

CHAPTER 12

The Seer Anointing
and Discerning Spiritual Beings

We are living in a day and age when God is opening people's eyes to see into spiritual realms. Part of this is going to be the ability to discern spiritual beings, both good and evil (Hebrews 5:14). Along with this will come an understanding that we can co-labor with the Holy Spirit to activate God's angels and that we have authority over angels of darkness—demons. As you move in this (also called the seer anointing), you will see the good stuff but you will also be aware of the bad stuff. But remember, God has given you all authority over these things—to cast them out, to step on them, to trample on them.

It is not a bad thing to see demonic entities (spiritual beings) and demonic devices or weapons. Because when God allows you to see them, you can take authority over them and rebuke them from operating in your sphere in influence. For instance, if someone in your family is troubled by addiction and you see that demon upon them (often in the form of an ugly little monkey-type thing, a snake, or a vice) and the Lord gives you a sword in the spiritual realm so you can cut off the head of that thing, what is going to happen? That person is going to get set free. They are going to be delivered from addiction in a supernatural way! Why do you think that Jesus gave you *all authority* over unclean spirits (spiritual beings)?

Look at Matthew 10:1: *"When He had called His twelve disciples to Him, He (Jesus) gave them power over unclean spirits, to cast them out, and to heal all kinds of sickness and all kinds of disease."* (See also Luke 9:1; 10:19.) The Lord gives you this same kind of delegated power and authority over the demonic realm. Why? To cast devils out and to heal the sick. This is another important subtlety of the seer anointing. When you begin to operate in the seer anointing, there will be a great increase in your grace gift and anointing to heal the sick. You will have the authority to discern or "see" demons associated with sickness and infirmity and then to cast them out and thereby heal *all* kinds of sickness and *all* kinds of disease. It's simple, and this dynamic of the seer anointing *is* available to you! Just believe to receive and take it by faith!

Once you begin to see in the spirit, you will need to learn to grow and mature in this aspect of the seer anointing (deliverance and healing). This aspect of the seer anointing may also come as a learning curve and in the process of time. That is perfectly OK; just embrace the journey. However, you may wish to seek out a ministry that is anointed in the seer realm. Seek to learn from seers as the Lord leads you. Remember, the Lord is raising up many "eagle nests" at this hour with those who will be anointed to train and equip God's seers (that means you). As you begin to operate in the seer anointing, the Lord will begin to reveal revelatory knowledge to you. This will help you to advance His Kingdom and walk in a new level of maturity and power. As I said before, the gift of the seer anointing is comparable to the golden eagle; it is a mature level of the prophetic anointing. It is the day and the hour that we live in that allows us to step into this aspect of God's Kingdom.

Hidden Mysteries Revealed

I believe that we are living in an amazing hour when the God of the universe is revealing secret and hidden mysteries and revelations to His friends.

> *And He* [Jesus] *said, "To you it has been given to know the* **mysteries** *of the* **kingdom of God**, *but to the rest it is given in*

parables, that 'Seeing they may not see, And hearing they may not understand'" (Luke 8:10, emphasis added).

The word *mysteries* in this passage means divine revelatory knowledge, secret things, things of great value hidden in the spiritual realm (like golf ball size diamonds). I shared with you before how people can be born again yet never enter into the weightier matters of God. They struggle their whole life even though they are Christians and will go to heaven. They never overcome poverty or they never overcome infirmity for they never walk in a higher revelatory knowledge of God. However, God wants you to *see and understand* the hidden and mysterious things in His Kingdom. I believe that we can all walk in supernatural health (see Psalm 103:5).

*For nothing is **secret** that will not be revealed, nor anything hidden that will not be **known** and come to light. Therefore take heed how you hear* (Luke 8:17-18, emphasis added).

In this scripture Jesus is talking about spiritual senses. There is more than one way to hear; you can hear with your natural ears but you can also hear and discern with your spirit. Remember, you can close your eyes and see with your ears. Close your eyes and say these words out loud, "Rose." What did you see? Did you see a rose or bouquet of flowers? Did you see a single rose? Then you have just seen with your ears.

We are living in a day and an hour when God is revealing secret things. The word *secret* used in this scripture above means concealed, kept in a private place. Do you have secrets you don't want to share with everybody? There are some things that you want to keep private and that you only share with your closest friends. God has treasure troves of things like this too. He has secrets and hidden mysteries that He only shares with His friends. We need to be diligent to become true friends of God. This is another key that can help activate the seer anointing and the unction of the Holy Spirit in your life.

Remember, one of the keys to stepping into the seer anointing is having intimacy and communion with God and becoming His friend. *"I no longer call you servants....Instead, I have called you friends"* (John 15:15, NIV). God reveals revelatory knowledge to His friends.

The word *known* in Luke 8:17 is *ginesko* in the Greek. It means to have a supernatural revelation of something, to understand a spiritual principle within your spirit. This scriptural dynamic has to do with our ability to see and hear into the spirit realm and to comprehend the reality of Christ's Kingdom that is all around us. This is what the seer anointing and the ability to see, hear, smell, taste, touch, and understand things from the spiritual realm is all about.

In Luke 8:18 Jesus when tells us, *"Take heed how you hear,"* He is teaching about this same principle. We are living in a day and an hour when God is activating our spiritual senses to "hear" in a new way.

Spiritually Blind and Deaf

In Matthew 13:14-15, the Lord quotes an Old Testament scripture from Isaiah. This is one of the few quotes that is in all four Gospels (see also Mark 4:12; Luke 8:10; John 12:40), which earmarks these scriptures from Isaiah 6:9-10 as significant and crucial for us to understand. These scriptures from Isaiah are vital to understanding and unlocking the mysteries of the seer anointing in your life. I encourage you to meditate upon them consistently. Seek the Lord in prayer asking Him to help you to hear and understand and to see and to discern and perceive. (Actually, praying this is asking the Lord to unlock the seer anointing in your life.)

> *And He* [God] *said, "Go, and tell this people:* **'Keep on hearing, but do not understand; Keep on seeing, but do not perceive.'** *Make the heart of this people dull, And their ears heavy, And shut their eyes; Lest they see with their eyes, And hear with their ears, And understand with their heart, And return and be healed"* (Isaiah 6:9-10, emphasis added).

Remember, the Lord wants us to be seers. The Lord is telling us that there can be times that we don't really see the way that He wants us to see and we don't know how to hear the way that He wants us to hear. (Remember when I was in heaven and Jesus told me to see and then to hear repeatedly? I believe that was a parabolic portrait of Isaiah 6:9-10. Jesus desires for us to see and hear in a supernatural way. He desperately desires for His people to become mature seers.)

What the Lord is talking about in Isaiah 6 is that people do not spiritually see or hear very well in the heavenly realms. They are spiritually deaf and dumb. God wants us to hear; God wants us to be set free. It is our good fortune to discover the hidden and mysterious things in the Kingdom of God. Isaiah 6:9-10 is also parabolic. *Parabolic* means resembling a parable. Why should I consider it unusual for the Lord to speak to me today in parables?

Washed in His Blood

Think about Revelation 1:5-6: *"Jesus Christ, the faithful witness, the firstborn from the dead, and the ruler over the kings of the earth. To Him who loved us and washed us from our sins in His own blood, and has made us kings and priests to His God and Father, to Him be glory and dominion forever and ever."* Why did Jesus wash us in His blood? To make us kings and priests.

Look at Revelation 5:9-10: *"And they* [the living creatures and the twenty-four elders] *sang a new song, saying: 'You are worthy to take the scroll, And to open its seals; For You were slain, And have redeemed us to God by Your blood Out of every tribe and tongue and people and nation, And have made us kings and priests to our God; And we shall reign on the earth.'"*

We are talking about the mantle of Melchizedek. Jesus Christ, the High Priest of our confession, ripped and rended open the heavens and ascended into the heavenly realms. He was a forerunner; He prepared the way for those to follow after Him. He prepared a way for us to crack open the spiritual realm (open heaven) so that we could step into the heavenly realm. How can we do this? By having our spiritual senses activated, matured by reason of use (Hebrews 5:14).

Proverbs 25:2 tells us, *"It is the glory of God to conceal a matter, But the glory of kings is to search out a matter."* Revelation 5:10 tells us *we* are those kings. As kings and priests *we* are called to search out a matter. It has been granted to you and me to have revelations (plural) of the mysteries of the Kingdom of Heaven.

> *He answered and said to them, "Because it has been given to you to know the **mysteries** of the **kingdom of heaven**, but to them it has not been given"* (Matthew 13:11, emphasis added).

The "mysteries of the kingdom of heaven" could be defined as the truth of the Kingdom of Heaven, the truth or reality of the Gospel, or the reality of the true Gospel. How can we know these mysteries? It's because God opens up our spiritual eyes and all of our spiritual senses and the unction of the Holy One is activated in our lives and our spirit man becomes dominate within us in terms of perception. We learn to be led by our regenerated spirits and the Spirit of the Lord, rather than by our carnal minds or our souls.

The seer anointing and the unction of the Holy Spirit enables us to know, see, or discern the hidden mysteries of the Kingdom of Heaven. At times this can include spiritual beings, both good and evil. When this process begins to accelerate in our lives, we are actually being transformed into mature sons and daughters of the Most High God. In the next chapter we will look at your calling to develop into mature sons and daughters of the Kingdom of Heaven and operate in maturity as a seer.

CHAPTER 13

Creation Is Ready for the Revealing of the Sons and Daughters of God

For as many as are led by the Spirit of God, these are sons of God. For you did not receive the spirit of bondage again to fear, but you received the Spirit of adoption by whom we cry out, "Abba, Father" (Romans 8:14-15).

When we are led by the Spirit of God, we are the sons or daughters of God. How did we get there? Because God did not want for you to receive the spirit of bondage again to fear. Fear, particularly the fear of man, can hold us back from moving into the deeper things of God. If we are going to step into the seer anointing, if we are going to be mature sons and daughters of God, we need to understand that we do not have a spirit of bondage or fear but we have a spirit of adoption. God is our Abba Father. He has given us a spirit of adoption, a spirit where we can come and sit in Daddy's lap. That's a spirit where we know His love personally.

If my daughter makes a mistake, I don't chastise. I say, "Oh, come here. Let's talk about that. Let me love on you." If she has a cut on her finger, I say, "Come here. Let's heal that wound." You may have wounds that need healing. The Lord wants you to come into His presence and let Him heal those wounds. He wants you to know Him as a friend.

When we are led by our soul, mind, will, and emotions (our flesh), we have a dull heart, heavy ears, and blinded eyes. It does not matter how long you have been saved and it does not matter how much you go to church; if you are a carnal Christian, you are spiritually deaf, dumb, and blind. But God wants for you to see and hear from Him clearly. He wants you to know Him as Abba Father who is ready to give you good gifts. The Father wants you to be totally and completely healed.

> *If you then, being evil, know how to give good gifts to your children, how much more will your Father who is in heaven give good things to those who ask Him!* **(**Matthew 7:11**)**.

What things would He give us? Hidden secrets in God's Kingdom. Ask Him for some hidden mysteries. Ask Him for some hidden treasures. In the third book of my trilogy I write about the crystal clear waters of Psalm 23 where there are treasures that we can take. I would rest at the feet of Jesus and then go swimming in the river. Besides the fish that I enjoyed finding, I found a treasure chest. I would pull gemstones from the treasure chest there and bring them up and show them to Jesus. He was delighted and gave me a pouch to put them in. Every time I would find a gemstone in the heavenly realms, when I returned to earth I would have new revelation about the word of God. I would know things beyond my human understanding.

This is a wonderful benefit of activating the seer anointing in your life. Your ability to see and hear from the Lord will greatly increase, and your intimacy and communion with the Lord will grow into a very special treasure. *The Lord will give you the seer anointing when you ask Him in faith.*

> *Do not fear, little flock, for it is your Father's good pleasure to give you the kingdom* (Luke 12:32).

Do you know what makes Papa God happy? When you step into the Kingdom; when you have the unction of the Holy Spirit activated in your life. When your spiritual senses are matured by reason of use, you begin to taste, smell, touch, hear, and ascend into the heavenly realms to see and to have God speak to you clearly. It makes Papa God happy. It's His good pleasure to give us the Kingdom. It's amazing! Think about it!

Many people live in spiritual ignorance. They are led by their soul and flesh and cannot see or comprehend spiritual things. We are living in a day and hour when we cannot afford to live our lives in spiritual deafness and blindness. We can't do this anymore. It's too critical of an hour.

Isaiah 26:3 is a beautiful promise: "*You will keep him in perfect peace Whose mind is stayed on You, Because he trusts in You.*" There is a fear that's loosed in the world. There's an ungodly doctrine in the church that says we need to dig a hole, live in a cave, learn how to grow crops, and eat taters. Now, if God's telling you to do that, you better do that. But according to my Bible, Jesus overcame the devil; and if I'm living in a right relationship with Him, He'll supply all of my needs according to His riches in glory (Philippians 4:19). You'll have exactly what you want. The enemy is trying to release fear on the Body of Christ; but God wants to release our faith into the heavenly realms. God wants us to rise above the confusion and conflicts of the present world.

Why do you need the seer anointing? Because you need to see and hear from the heavenly realms for yourself, as it's important in this day and hour. Why? I wrote about 20/20 vision, referring to 2 Chronicles 20:20 where it tells us we need to believe God's prophets. But you need to hear God for yourself. One of the ways you can do that is by maturing your spiritual senses by reason of use to see and hear what God is saying for your own personal situation. If you allow someone else to hear God for you, you are in a very unhealthy place, especially in this day and hour.

Ezekiel 13:1-2 tells us, "*And the word of the Lord came to me, saying, 'Son of man, prophesy against the prophets of Israel who prophesy, and say to those who prophesy out of their own heart.'*" Remember, we have spirit, soul, and body. What is our heart? It's our soul—our mind, will, and emotions. *"Hear the word of the Lord! Thus says the Lord God: 'Woe to the foolish prophets, who follow their own spirit and have seen nothing!'"* (vv. 2-3). We need to see what God is doing if we are going to prophesy.

If you are really hearing God, there should be power accompanying your word. A lot of people prophesy but there is no power. If they are speaking words that are not from the Lord, they are taking the Lord's name in vain; breaking one of the Ten Commandments spoken of in Exodus 7:20. If their words are the words of God, they should be doing the work of Jesus. If they don't have this fruit in their lives, they prophesy out of their own spirit (soul) and have "seen" nothing. These kinds of prophets may be backslidden.

Ezekiel goes on in verses 4-8: *"'O Israel, your prophets are like foxes in the deserts. You have not gone up into the gaps to build a wall for the house of Israel to stand in battle on the day of the Lord. They have envisioned futility and false divination, saying, "Thus says the Lord!" But the Lord has not sent them; yet they hope that the word may be confirmed. Have you not seen a futile vision, and have you not spoken false divination? You say, "The Lord says," but I have not spoken.' Therefore thus says the Lord God: 'Because you have spoken nonsense and envisioned lies,* [they didn't actually see what God was doing; they spoke out of their own heart, their soul] *therefore I am indeed against you,' says the Lord God."* Who is He against? The prophets.

In verse 9 the Lord says, *"My hand will be against the prophets who envision futility and who divine lies; they shall not be in the assembly of My people, nor be written in the record of the house of Israel."* He continues to rebuke the prophets through the remainder of chapter 13 and into chapter 14.

Hear my heart. I'm all for 2 Chronicles 20:20; we need to hear God's prophets. There are some prophets who I listen to faithfully. But I also get on my knees and ask God myself about prophetic words. Any prophetic word that you receive should only confirm what God has already spoken to you personally Spirit to spirit.

In Ezekiel 14 God speaks to the children of Israel: *"Therefore say to the house of Israel, 'Thus says the Lord God: 'Repent, turn away from your idols.'"* What idols is He talking about? The prophets. *"'Turn your faces away from all your abominations. For anyone of the house of Israel, or of the strangers who dwell in Israel, who separates himself from Me and sets up his idols in his heart and puts before him what causes him to stumble into iniquity, then comes to a prophet to inquire of him concerning Me, I the Lord will answer him by Myself. I will set My face against that man* [who sought a prophetic word] *and make him a sign and a proverb, and I will cut him off from the midst of My people. Then you shall know that I am the Lord. And if the prophet is induced to speak anything, I the Lord have induced that prophet, and I will stretch out My hand against him and destroy him'"* (vv. 6-9). Ezekiel goes on to talk about how God will speak through the prophets according to the multitude of idols in our hearts.

When we allow fear to rule and reign in the Body of Christ, it becomes an idol. And God is going to speak to us through the multitude of idols in our hearts. Fear is not trusting God; it is a lack of faith. If we don't have faith in God to protect us, what we really do is bring the finished work of Jesus Christ and the Cross to no effect. Jesus either died upon the Cross to give us life, or He didn't. He brought us total salvation—prosperity, health, and salvation for our spirits.

Therefore, if people are functioning out of fear, God is going to speak through His prophets and give them prophesies that are fearful and inaccurate. He is going to speak according to the multitude of idols in their hearts. So we must not believe every word we hear the prophets speak. We must test all things. If you find this offensive, seek the Lord diligently and check your heart.

If you are going to step into the seer realm, you need to mature spiritually. Part of becoming mature sons and daughters of God and having the seer anointing activated in your life is to be able to see and hear God for yourself; not to depend on the prophets to hear God for you. How is that going to happen? You begin to see and hear what God is doing. You cannot do this in the flesh; it is your recreated spirit that discerns and hears God. In the next chapter we will look at more scriptural principles that help us to overcome our flesh and learn to hear God's voice more clearly as individuals.

CHAPTER 14

Inheriting the Kingdom of God

It is only through our spirit man that we can activate the seer anointing in our lives and learn to hear clearly for ourselves as individuals.

> **Flesh and blood** *cannot inherit the Kingdom of God; nor does corruption inherit incorruption* (1 Corinthians 15:50, emphasis added).

We cannot perceive the Kingdom with our carnal minds; we cannot see, taste, touch, smell, or inherit the Kingdom of God with our minds and souls. It is only through our spirit man that we can access the grace and anointing of Jesus Christ (the Messiah or anointed One) that is available to us in this day and hour.

> *For all that is in the world—the lust of the flesh, the lust of the eyes, and the pride of life—is not of the Father but is of the world* (1 John 2:16).

God is a Spirit and the Holy Spirit communicates and speaks to us Spirit to spirit. To enter into the Kingdom of God, you enter by your recreated spirit.

Allowing idols in your heart will hinder you from hearing God clearly. We need to search our hearts to see if we have idols in there. We are supposed to walk in health; we are supposed to walk in the fullness of Christ's atonement. But sometimes we fall short. Why is that? Sometimes it is because of the multitude of the idols that we have in our heart. Fear can be an idol; also anything that is more important to you than God can be an idol. Family can become an idol. Ministry can be an idol. Money can be an idol. Your home can be an idol. Your job can be an idol. Prophecy can be an idol. We must examine our hearts and release all the idols that have taken up residence there.

A "Word" About the Prophets

We need to understand about the different types of prophetic anointing. We already discussed the *nabi* prophet and the seer prophet. First I want to make it clear that I do honor *God's* prophets as it tells us in Psalm 105:15: "*Do not touch My anointed ones, And do My prophets no harm.*" I recognize the prophets and I honor the prophets. That being said, I would like to discuss 2 Chronicles 20:20 where Jehoshaphat is speaking:

> *Jehoshaphat stood and said, "Hear me, O Judah and you inhabitants of Jerusalem: Believe in the Lord your God, and you shall be established; believe His prophets, and you shall prosper."*

Remember, 20:20 speaks of 20/20 vision. This book is about unlocking the seer anointing, and in order to do that we must have our spiritual eyes opened and to have perfect vision. And that's what the above scripture is all about.

Jehoshaphat is addressing Judah and the inhabitants of Jerusalem; prophetically that means the church. Then he says, "*Believe in the Lord your God, and you shall be established.*" The word translated "established" means to be supported, to be fostered, to be cared for, to have assurance, to have peace or safety, or to rest or trust in safety or a safe place. So when we believe in the Lord, we come into a place of intimacy and protection. And then he says, "*Believe His prophets, and you shall prosper.*" The word translated "prophets" is *nabi*— God-inspired man or word prophet. The word translated "prosper" means to push forward as with labor, to break out of a hard place, to be profitable, or to be prosperous (usually by the sweat of your brow and the labor of your hands, not through the supernatural grace of God).

Jehoshaphat is giving options here. Plan A is to believe the Lord your God and come into a place of rest. Plan B is to listen to the prophets and prosper; but that's a place of work, a place of the flesh, a place of breaking out and breaking through. So 2 Chronicles 20:20 is about birth of vision (seer anointing). You need to be able to see the Lord and hear the Lord for yourself.

Do we need to listen to God's prophets? Absolutely! I listen to God's prophets; some I listen to very carefully. But the promise is that if we know the Lord, we will be in a safe place of rest; if we hear the Lord for ourselves, we are in a better place than if we merely hear the prophets. For example, if I look through another man's glasses my vision is not clear because the glasses are specific to that man's need.

Likewise, if I look through a prophet's "glasses"—his prophetic revelation, his knowledge, his understanding—it won't be clear to me. But when God speaks to me, I get clear revelation. When the seer anointing is activated in my life and I begin to see and hear Go for myself, I can have clear revelation about my individual situation. Instead of laboring to break out, I can rest in the Lord and prosper in a higher level. We need the prophets, but we must not become in bondage to them by being spiritually lazy and only hearing from the Lord through them. Learn to hear the voice of the Lord for yourself. There are many ways to learn to hear the voice of God.

On the Pneuma Network you can access our eleven-part teaching series on *The Eleven Ways God Is Speaking to You Today*. (This is a fifteen-hour audio sermon series on hearing the voice of the Lord.) You can find and easily launch the Pneuma Network from our web-page, www.kingofgloryministries.org. The Pneuma Network is a free teaching outreach of King of Glory Ministries International. You can also sign up to receive free monthly video, audio, and written sermons from the Pneuma Network by joining our mailing list on our homepage.

Idols in Our Hearts

God wants His people to hear His voice—clearly. Jesus promised that His sheep would hear His voice (see John 10:27). If we are not hearing God for ourselves and are depending on another man or another woman to hear God for us—no matter how anointed they are and no matter what office of ministry they hold, it is a dangerous thing because we could fall into idol worship.

We discussed Ezekiel 13:2 where God said He would be against the prophets (*nabi*) who prophesied "*out of their own heart*." We also studied God as a triune being—God the Father, God the Son, and God the Holy Spirit; and that we were created in God's image as a three-part being with a triune nature—body, soul, and spirit. Our "heart" is part of our soul—the mind, will, and emotions. So this scripture is saying that the prophets are prophesying from their intellect or their soul; they are not prophesying by the Spirit of God. It is possible that some of that is going on these days.

The idols in our hearts might even be our ministry or the gifts of the Spirit or miracles, signs, and wonders. Perhaps your idol may be the gifts of the Spirit like prophecy or the word of wisdom. Some of us have those idols in our heart because we have developed unhealthy relationships by putting *too much emphasis* on the prophets, ministry, and other spiritual gifts. Even the seer anointing could become an idol if we were to allow it. Sometimes we become lazy and become too dependent on hearing God through another man or woman of God. So I want to emphasize that this passage of Scripture is very timely for the Body of Christ at this hour. Consider asking the Holy Spirit to reveal to you any idols that have set up shop in your heart.

We need to pray and ask the Lord to remove any idols that are within our heart so we can have that 20/20 spiritual vision. We want to rise above the place where we must plow through because we get a prophetic word. We need to mature and grow into the place where we see God and hear well from the Lord *ourselves* and get our own breakthrough from the realms of heaven, stepping into a place of rest and prosperity.

Prayer for the Cleansing of the Heart

In Jesus name I thank You, Father, for everything You are doing. And, Lord, I thank You that You give Your children good gifts. I thank You that if I seek Your Kingdom, You will give me revelatory knowledge. Lord, I know that when I seek to have my eyes and ears activated, You will not give me a stone or a scorpion; You will give me the Kingdom of God. In the name of Jesus Christ of Nazareth, I am asking You for Your good gifts. I am asking that You open up my eyes to see and open up my ears to hear. Lord, forgive me if I have allowed prophecy, prophets, or other spiritual gifts to become idols in my heart. I repent for these things now.

Lord, I ask You to search my heart. I ask that You would take from me idols of fear, idols of unbelief, idols of doubt, or un-Christlike beliefs that might dominate my heart. Show me any areas, any hidden agendas within my heart, that are not in tune with You and that would hinder me from hearing You clearly, God. I ask that You would reveal them to me. Show me anything that would inhibit me from receiving the fullness of the anointing to see, any hindrance or roadblock that would keep me from stepping into the fullness of Your Kingdom. Bring to my remembrance anything that would prevent me from entering into the deep things of God. If I have made unrighteous judgments against others or if the words of my mouth or the meditations of my heart have been unacceptable in Your sight, Lord, I ask that You would reveal them to me now.

As I wait on You, Lord, and You show me the areas where I have sinned or fallen short, I ask that You would minister to me. By Your grace I do repent of those things with all of my heart. Please forgive me, Lord. Forgive me of strongholds or anything in my heart that is unacceptable to You. I beg You to create in me a clean heart and renew a steadfast spirit within me. Restore my soul. I thank You that You are setting me free.

Lord, I ask You to cover me in Your blood. Your word says in Isaiah 43:26 that if we put You in remembrance that You will contend with us. Your word says in Revelation 1:5-6 that the blood of Jesus makes us kings and priests. Lord, I thank You for the miracle of my purification. Lord, I thank You that You are preparing me to step into the fullness of the seer anointing. I give You all the praise and the honor and the glory for all that You are doing. I pray as King David did in Psalm 51:10, "Create in me a clean heart, O God, And renew a steadfast spirit within me."

Lord, I position myself to receive from the realms of heaven. I ask, Holy Spirit, that You would begin to speak to me. I thank You, Lord, that You are activating my ability to see and hear and taste and smell and touch and enter and inherit the Kingdom of God. I ask that You activate the gift of the seer anointing in my life. In the name of Jesus Christ of Nazareth, I pray. Amen.

In the next chapter we will look at more scriptural principles that can help us mature and learn how to use our weapons of spiritual warfare more effectively in the seer realm.

CHAPTER 15

The Weapons of Our Warfare—
"Shield Up!"

If you are really serious about stepping into the seer realm, you need to be covered in the blood of Jesus and be in right relationship with God. This is because the enemy of your soul does not want you to see and does not want you to hear what God has ordained for you to do. The devil wants to keep you spiritually deaf and dumb. Your adversary does not want you to be able to discern the evil and nefarious schemes he is seeking to perpetrate. So when you begin to step into the seer anointing, you can expect warfare. Praise God for warfare because that means you are on the right track!

As we mature in the seer anointing, we will begin to grow in our spiritual ability to discern both good and evil. It is crucial for the Body of Christ to mature and develop godly discernment at this hour. Godly discernment will help to ensure that the approaching outpourings of revival will not be contaminated with the unholy leaven of witchcraft and other ungodly self-centered agendas. We see godly discernment outlined in Hebrews 5:14.

Exercising Your Spiritual Senses

Look at Hebrews 5:14: "*Solid food* [the hidden or mysterious principles or weightier matters of God's Kingdom] *belongs to those who are of full age, that is, those who by reason of use have their senses exercised to discern both good and evil.*"

We can grow and mature our spiritual senses in the same way that a weight lifter builds his biceps as we "build up" or exercise our spiritual senses seeking to comprehend the spiritual elements of the Kingdom of God.

Many people have shared with me that they see "flashes" or "streams of light" and have thought they might be seeing angelic activity or were beginning to see into the spirit. Many times when you "get a feeling" you are beginning to see or discern the spiritual realms, you are! You may just need to massage your spiritual senses and the seer gift to step into the realm of the spirit. This will help you to begin to see or discern the spiritual activity that is already unfolding around you.

If you are seeing "flashes" or "streams of light," a simple prayer can help activate your gift of discerning of spirits and the seer anointing in your life. Activating the gift of discerning of spirits in your life can be as simple as taking a step of faith and asking the Lord for it. Ask! Activating the seer anointing or your ability to discern or perceive angelic activity can be that simple.

> *Ask, and it will be given to you; seek, and you will find; knock, and it will be opened to you* (Matthew 7:7).

Remember, it does not matter through which of your five senses that the seer anointing begins to operate; they are all valid. You can be released or activated into seer anointing and into the gift of discerning of spirits through any one of your five senses (visual sight, hearing, touch, smell, and taste). Remember, you can "learn to discern" with all five of your traditional senses. I have written dozens of testimonies about times when the seer anointing has manifested in the lives of people who discerned angelic activity through each of these physical senses in my *Dancing with Angels* trilogy.

In this important passage of Scripture (Hebrews 5:14), the phrase "*solid food*" can be interpreted to mean the weightier, more advanced revelations, or understanding the hidden mysteries of the Kingdom of Heaven. These hidden mysteries are revealed to those who are "*of full age*," meaning those who have grown into maturity, who have developed a higher or more advanced ability to see and perceive spiritual matters. This passage is referring to those who have been diligent to work and develop spiritual discernment by exercising their spiritual senses, such as the seer anointing. Remember that the gift of discerning of spirits can be considered to be an aspect of the seer anointing.

We are talking about the ability to discern between *"both good and evil"*—godly and demonic, heavenly and wicked. Therefore, in the next part of this book I want to take some time and illustrate some examples of how you will be able to discern between godly and demonic beings (angels and demons), as well as heavenly and wicked spiritual things (both good and evil). These will be basic examples and testimonies of how the seer anointing will unfold and can activate in your life. Let's start by beginning to study the importance and reality of your weapons of warfare found in the Scriptures. Spiritual weapons of warfare are some of the good and evil things that you will learn to discern. As a seer you will need to constantly take up the armor of God found in Ephesians 6.

> *Put on the whole armor of God, that you may be able to stand against the wiles of the devil. For we do not wrestle against flesh and blood, but against principalities, against powers, against the rulers of the darkness of this age, against spiritual hosts of wickedness in the heavenly places* (Ephesians 6:11-12).

What is this scripture talking about standing against? Spiritual beings—demons. Paul understood this stuff. This is what is defined as the basic tenets or elementary principles of the Christian faith found in Hebrews 6:1-3. I suggest that you invest time meditating upon Hebrews 6. Sometimes demons and demonic plans work through other people, including Christians, to spew vile accusations and to perpetrate evil agendas. When the seer anointing activates in your life, you will begin to discern these evil things more readily (words and word curses can be weapons of the enemy). "Shield up! Armor on!"

"Therefore take up the whole armor of God, that you may be able to withstand in the evil day, and having done all, to stand" (Ephesians 6:13).

Stand Still and Let God Work for You

Sometimes you just need to stand firm. You don't need to go back, you just need to stand firm until the pneuma of God—the breath of God, *ruah ha-qodesh*, the Holy Spirit—and the angels of God go before you and clear your path. As we learned earlier, a lot of people depend upon prophets and prophecy today. However, when we trust the prophets we have to press, we have to work, we have to get that breakthrough on the prophetic word by the sweat of our brow. However, you can get your breakthrough in a much easier way.

Learn to stand still, rest in the Lord, and wait for God so you can hear and see what He's doing (2 Chronicles 20:17). Then He sends His pneuma before us—His breath, His Spirit, *ruah ha-qodesh*—and His angels are released to work on our behalf (Genesis 24:7; Hebrews 1:14). So sometimes we just need to stand still and let God work on our behalf. We need to learn to discern good spiritual beings (God's angels) and just stand still and release them to work on our behalf.

"Stand therefore, having girded your waist with truth, having put on the breastplate of righteousness, and having shod your feet with the preparation of the gospel of peace; above all, taking the shield of faith" (Ephesians 6:14-16). "Shield up!"

Faith to Shield You

Do you need more faith to shield you? You were given a measure of faith when you were born again, and that's great; but there is another level of faith. Each of us has faith according to the measure of faith God gave us (Romans 12:3). But God can give us another measure of faith at any time. This can be a spiritual gift (1 Corinthians 12:9), a gift given by grace for a specific purpose or need. Pray to God that you will not only receive another measure of faith but also a release of the gift of faith because it can transform your life and help you walk in a deeper level of the seer anointing.

Why do you need both of these? *"Above all, taking the shield of faith with which you will be able to quench all the fiery darts* [evil or demonic weapons] *of the wicked one. And take the helmet of salvation, and the sword of the Spirit, which is the word of God"* (Ephesians 6:16-17). "Shield up!"

The Lord has given me a really amazing spiritual sword (by faith). I first saw my spiritual sword in the seer realms. I've used this weapon of spiritual warfare to lop off the head of many demons. I see it all very clearly in the spirit. Because I have walked in these things for over a decade, the things of the spirit are becoming more real to me than the things in the world. There will be times when the seer anointing will manifest and begin to operate in my spirit and my spirit man goes on "high alert." My spirit is alerted to evil or demonic entities and the evil plans that are unfolding around me.

Pay attention when this happens! This kind of seer revelation can be uncomfortable as you mature and the Lord begins to allow you to see and discern both the good and evil in people, places, and organizations. Sometimes you can discern evil attached to physical objects. Be careful of what you handle and what items you allow to come into your house. When you begin to discern and see the demonic realm manifesting through other Christians and people inside of the church, this can really be disappointing and disheartening. Most of the time people who allow demonic and evil things to work through them are totally ignorant to the fact that they are releasing demonic spirits and curses. They are spiritually deaf and blind (Isaiah 6:9-10).

People like this may be battling a religious spirit or religious demons. In some cases these demons are familiar spirits. Familiar spirits are often associated with generational curses. Many a time I have wanted to ask people in the church who allow demonic spirits to speak or pray through them a simple question: "Can you discern a religious spirit?" I don't ask, never have; but I assume that the answer would be no. You see, that is the sad thing about these kinds of sneaky demons. The people who are oppressed with demons like these often cannot discern them, as they are stuck in the sin of Romans 1:31—they are "undiscerning." They are usually spiritually deaf and blind. They are unable to distinguish the difference between good and evil (Isaiah 5:20).

Build Yourself Up

When warfare is coming against you, pray in the Holy Spirit. Build yourself up as the Scripture encourages us in Jude 20. There is a place when we pray in the Spirit where we speak directly to Abba Father. At this place the enemy will just flee because he doesn't understand what you are saying, except he knows that you are talking to Papa and he needs to get out of there. The breath of God—*ruah ha-qodesh*—could come at any second, so he flees. "*Resist the devil and he will flee from you*" (James 4:7). Praying in the Spirit is a great way to get rid of the devil or demons working through people. Praying in the Spirit is a powerful and wonderful weapon of our warfare to resist the devil and his minions. This is another supernatural key; you do not even have to pray out loud or audibly.

If you want to be blessed, pray for other people: "*Being watchful to this end with all perseverance and supplication for all the saints*" (Ephesians 6: 18). Pray for them to be healed. Pray for them to be set free. Pray for them to fulfill their God-ordained destiny completely 100 percent. Bless them with your prayers; ask God to bless them in every way.

There are many other really important warfare scriptures. Search the Scriptures and ask the Holy Spirit to reveal several warfare scriptures to you for your personal use; here are four:

For the weapons of our warfare are not carnal but mighty in God for pulling down strongholds (2 Corinthians 10:4).

Praying always with all prayer and supplication in the Spirit (Ephesians 6: 18).

But you, beloved, building yourselves up on your most holy faith, praying in the Holy Spirit, keep yourselves in the love of God, looking for the mercy of our Lord Jesus Christ unto eternal life (Jude 20-21).

No weapon formed against you shall prosper, And every tongue which rises against you in judgment You shall condemn. This is the heritage of the servants of the Lord, And their righteousness is from Me (Isaiah 54:17).

Evil Devices and Weapons

What weapon is formed against us? The enemy's devices (fiery darts); the devices of demonic beings in the spiritual realm. We are servants of the Most High God. So why do we sometimes experience warfare and at times the enemy's weapons seem to prosper against us? Maybe we have let our guard down. "Shield up!" Perhaps it is because we have not decreed God's word; it is the trigger for our supernatural weapons. Psalm 103:20 tells us, *"Bless the Lord, you His angels, Who excel in strength, who do His word, Heeding the voice of His word."* As we speak God's word, our spiritual weapons are fired. Sometimes we have not prayed in the Spirit as we should. (Look for my *31 Word Decree* book to help you be diligent with daily word confessions and helpful prayers).

Offensive Prayer

Father, I thank You that there is no weapon that is formed against me that shall prosper. Every tongue that is risen against me—incantations or word curses of witchcraft—I condemn. I command every religious spirit and every demon assigned to these word curses to loose your assignments immediately, in the mighty name of Jesus Christ of Nazareth. I bind every word curse that that has been spoken against me, and I condemn them now, because this is my authority and my inheritance as a servant of the Most High God. Amen!

Do you know what happens when you speak that out? God's angels recognize it. They know that it is the Father's word and they have to pay attention to it. Psalm 103:20 tells us the angels "heed" the word, it means they pay close attention and they run to perform it.

Isaiah 54:17 expresses a very important spiritual principle that we must not forget: God has given us the power and authority to command and condemn every word curse that is spoken against us. We have the authority to bind every demonic assignment associated with occult words or Christian witchcraft. In the next chapter we will investigate how you can deal in a godly manner with the witchcraft that you "see" and discern.

CHAPTER 16

The Seer Anointing
and Christian Witchcraft

Sometimes in the Body of Christ when Christians are praying for people, what they are really doing is cursing them with their words. That allows demonic beings to have access and liberty to operate. Sometimes we need to break off these word curses spoken by Christians, which is Christian witchcraft (white witchcraft). This same principle can also apply to many doctors' "diagnoses." Many times intercessors pray witchcraft prayers against God's people in ignorance. This is not pleasant to talk about, but it is true. Some of the things we have to battle against come from within the four walls of the church. (For more detailed teaching on this subject, get the resource *Overcoming the Accuser of the Brethren.* This audio sermon can set you free!)

Personally, I could write dozens of "horror stories" about times that Kathy and I have been forced to deal with witchcraft and witchcraft prayers in the church. However, since this is not edifying, I am going to resist the temptation to give you specific examples of discerning and dealing with witchcraft in the church. Most discerning ministers who have been in ministry for any length of time have similar "horror stories" of dealing with witchcraft. I am speaking not only about occult witchcraft, but I am also writing about and alerting you to white witchcraft, or Christian witchcraft.

Sometimes the most vile and nasty demonic spirits and nefarious evil agendas come against us from within the four walls of the church.

When you begin to develop your seer gifting, at times you will discern both. Unfortunately, a large percentage of churches, ministries, and ministers have absolutely no discernment in reference to witchcraft (both kinds) in the Body of Christ. Having said this, let me add that the Lord is well aware of the nefarious plans and witchcraft which people (wittingly and unwittingly) seek to release against His people. God's heart is that witches would be saved and that and those who unknowing operate in witchcraft would be set free and healed. This principle is spelled out in 2 Peter 3:9:

> *The Lord is not slack concerning His promise, as some count slackness, but is longsuffering toward us, not willing that any* [including occult witches and warlocks and those who unwittingly practice white witchcraft] *should perish but that all should come to repentance.*

Many people in the Body of Christ today are dealing with witchcraft and demonic opposition. And it is certain that when your seer gifting and discernment blossoms and you become mature in your ability to see and discern, you will become aware of both kinds of witchcraft. So, how can you react in a godly manner when the Lord begins to give you seer revelation and discernment concerning demonic and wicked activity in the Body of Christ?

The answer is that we must always utilize the seer gifting and discernment that God allows us to be stewards over, in, and through the love of God. I believe that discernment without God's love can at times be sinful. We must guard our hearts and not allow unrighteous judgments to have place in your lives (John 7:24). Remember what Paul warned us about in 1 Corinthians 13:1-8:

> *Though I speak with the tongues of men and of angels* [operate in spiritual gifts], *but have not love, I have become sounding brass or a clanging cymbal. And though I have the gift of prophecy, and understand all mysteries and all knowledge*

[operate in the seer anointing], *and though I have all faith, so that I could remove mountains, but have not love, I am nothing. And though I bestow all my goods to feed the poor, and though I give my body to be burned, but have not love, it profits me nothing. Love suffers long and is kind; love does not envy; love does not parade itself, is not puffed up; does not behave rudely, does not seek its own, is not provoked, thinks no evil; does not rejoice in iniquity, but rejoices in the truth; bears all things, believes all things, hopes all things, endures all things. Love never fails.*

The seer anointing and the gift of discerning of spirits will increase in your life as you mature. This maturity comes as you are diligent to exercise your spiritual senses according to the principle of Hebrews 5:14. As this dynamic unfolds in your life, you will come to a place where you will begin to discern both good and evil. In fact, as the seer anointing develops in your life, at times you will see both good and evil. As I wrote earlier, at times you will see and discern evil and wickedness in the Body of Christ. This can be very uncomfortable. For many Christians this is a forbidden subject.

Many churches and ministries choose to ignore witchcraft. In fact, in many churches the subject of witchcraft is taboo. They would rather ignore it and hope that the witchcraft and demonic realm operating in the church and in the Body of Christ would just "go away." It is also possible that they may be ignorant to the presence of witchcraft. But remember, the Scripture is clear on this subject. We are called to resist the devil (James 4:7). I, for one, am thankful that God is raising up seers to reveal, resist, and overcome this darkness and evil in a scriptural and godly way. This will help to set many people free from heavy yokes of darkness and curses of witchcraft. So, as uncomfortable as this subject may be, I am addressing it here: witchcraft will definitely be something that you will "bump into" as you grow and mature in your seer gifting and the gift of discerning of spirits.

Binding the devil

At times intercessors can be unwittingly used by the powers of darkness to pray ungodly prayers over and into a church or ministry. At other times leadership can allow people who are not mature in their gifting to pray for others in their church or ministry. Sometimes people who are on the "ministry team" have not submitted fully to the Holy Spirit's sanctification. Therefore, they may have "issues" or "open doors" from their past that allow demonic spirits to operate through them as they pray and lay hands upon people. In instances like this there can be an unholy transfer of demonic things. Some people call this kind of demonic impartation "getting slimed."

That is why we do not allow just anyone to pray or prophesy over the saints who attend our Moravian Falls Heaven Touching Earth Gatherings. We have a ministry team selected from those who have submitted to our ministry and with whom we have a strong relationship. We know their character, and all of our ministry team members have been with us for at least one year. They must all comply with our ministry team guidelines, and they agree to abide by these godly principles as they give personal ministry. This helps us to ensure that all ministry in our conferences is released decently and in order (1 Corinthians 14:40). In this way we resist the devil and train our ministry teams to grow in the character Christ, the anointing of the Holy Spirit, and in godly discernment.

You should always be careful who you allow to lay hands upon you and pray and prophesy over you. "Shield up!"

As you grow and mature in your seer anointing and discernment, there will be times when you will be given a "high alert" from the Holy Spirit. This kind of spiritual "high alert" can go off when there is witchcraft in operation. I always tell my wife, Kathy, to keep her shield up the week before we travel to a new city or place to minister. Because that is an opportune time when the enemy will seek to distract you and "slime" you through other people who exude evil and witchcraft, whether knowingly or unknowingly. This type of "high alert" is actually a function of the unction of the Holy Spirit that releases revelation to you about the presence of evil. I call this type of discernment the "Astro anointing." When the "Astro anointing" bubbles up in our spirit, it should be a "red flag." "Ruh roh! Shield up!

Here is some background for the younger seers reading this. Astro was a character on the cartoon program *The Jetsons. The Jetsons* was an animated series produced by Hanna-Barbara that aired on television from the early 1960s through the '80s. George Jetson was the main character. His family included his wife, Jane Jetson, his teenage daughter, Judy, and his son, Elroy. Elroy had a big goofy, harebrained dog named Astro. When Astro would break something, cause another catastrophe, or when another hilarious calamity was about to happen, he was would always say, "Ruh roh" meaning "Uh oh!" Astro spoke with a little speech impediment. "Ruh roh" is something that bubbles up in my spirit when my seer gift goes on "high alert." The "Astro anointing" can happen at any place at any time. "Ruh roh! Shield up!"

God Has Given Us Power and Authority

"Scottie, get the photon torpedoes activated and ready to fire!" "Shields up!"

"Fire away!"

> *Father, I thank You that there is no weapon that is formed against me that shall prosper. Every tongue that is risen against me—incantations or word curses of witchcraft—I condemn. I command every religious spirit and every demon assigned to these word curses to loose your assignments immediately, in the mighty name of Jesus Christ of Nazareth. I bind every word curse that that has been spoken against me and I condemn them now, because I have authority and this is inheritance as a servant of the Most High God. Amen!*

God has given us the power and authority to command or condemn every word curse that is spoken against us and to bind every demonic assignment that is associated with those curses. There is no need to be concerned when you begin to perceive evil things (even when you discern them in the church). You have all authority over them (Luke 9:1). *"A curse without cause shall not alight"* (Proverbs 26:2). Stay in the glory and purpose in your heart to walk in God's love no matter what!

Remember to always keep yourself covered in the blood of Jesus. Also, do not forget to enforce your spiritual boundaries by utilizing the powerful weapons found in the Scriptures. These are important scriptural keys that can help you to stay protected as you learn to grow and mature in the seer anointing. When the seer anointing begins to activate in your life, you will begin to discern unkind and evil thoughts and nefarious schemes, even in the Body of Christ. During times like these it is best to seek to walk in God's love and grace. Like Jesus, purpose in your heart to walk in nobility and humility.

Guard Your Heart Against False Discernment

Sometimes, through poor discernment, we can bring a curse and the righteous judgments of God upon ourselves. "Ruh roh!" So be careful that you judge righteously. Because *unrighteous judgments* will quench the flow of the seer anointing in your life! You can also ask the Lord to send you a godly apostolic leader with whom you can confidentially share such seer revelation. You need to be accountable to spiritual authority, or you will not have legitimate spiritual authority.

Accountability is a very important reason to be submitted to spiritual authority. Seek their sage advice and wisdom before taking any action concerning the evil that you may "see" and discern besides interceding for the person and or situation. The best course of action may be to keep your discernment to yourself until you are fully mature in your gifting. Most of the time the Lord gives you revelation like this to privately pray in secret for a person's healing or freedom.

Most of the time you are not called to share what the Spirit reveals to you with another human, only with God as you pray it back to Him in intercession. Too often intercessory prayer meetings turn into gossip, murmuring, and complaining sessions, as immature Christians begin to share their "revelations" they have "discerned" about people, pastors, and situations. Sometimes people operate in *false discernment*. This kind of discernment is not the fruit of the Spirit.

It is *deception from demonic spirits* that are masquerading as the Holy Spirit; this discernment is false. We need to guard our hearts against allowing gossip and ungodly murmurings and false discernment from entering into our spirit. Because when we listen to those things, we become guilty of the same sin as the one speaking them. It would be wise to remember that God hates this kind of evil—false discernment.

We see this in Proverbs 6:16-19:

> *These six things the Lord hates, Yes, seven are an abomination to Him: A proud look, A lying tongue, Hands that shed innocent blood, A heart that devises wicked plans, Feet that are swift in running to evil,* **A false witness who speaks lies, And one who sows discord among brethren** (emphasis added).

Philippians 4:8 is another scriptural key that can prevent you from falling into this trap of the devil:

> *Finally, brethren, whatever things are true, whatever things are noble, whatever things are just, whatever things are pure, whatever things are lovely, whatever things are of good report, if there is any virtue and if there is anything praiseworthy-- meditate on these things.*

Before you speak and share any seer discernment that deals with another person, judge it through the lens of Philippians 4:8. If it is not just, pure, lovely, virtuous, and praiseworthy, then just don't speak it out loud. Don't listen to words other speak that sow discord among the church and God's people; because if you do, you may be opening the door for sin and the demonic realm to have the legal right to oppress you (Genesis 4:7). This is especially true when the words (curses) being spoken are about a pastor or other minister (especially the Lord's prophets). This is particularly dangerous as you come under the righteous judgment of Psalm 105:15, *"Do not touch My anointed ones, And do My prophets no harm."*

Binding the Witchdoctor

Once, when Kathy and I moved to East Africa to host seven crusade meetings in seven cities, we were given an unusual greeting. During our first night in the nation, a witchdoctor had left us a little token. There hanging on a tree in front of our little bungalow was a dead black bird with fetishes and blood dripping from its body. The message was clear: "We know who you are. We know where you are. And we are going to kill you." (You see, a dead black bird of this kind is a death fetish, considered to be a magical object that is commonly used by witchdoctors in Africa when they are cursing a person.) At least some witchdoctors are open in their evil schemes! This is an example of how an object can have evil attached to it.

We could have panicked. But this was an Astro moment! "Ruh roh!" "Shield up!" We began to cover ourselves in the blood of Jesus and "fire away" our spiritual weapons of warfare: "Scottie, get the photon torpedoes activated and ready to fire!" And, "Shield up!"

By the way, we were privileged to lead an estimated 19,000 new believers to Jesus Christ as Lord and Savior during our missions trip, including a few witches and witchdoctors!

"Fire away!"

Father, I thank You that there is no weapon that is formed against me that shall prosper. Every tongue that is risen against me—incantations or word curses of witchcraft—I condemn. I command every religious spirit and every demon assigned to these word curses to loose your assignments immediately, in the mighty name of Jesus Christ of Nazareth. I bind every word curse that that has been spoken against me and I condemn them now, because I have authority and this is inheritance as a servant of the Most High God. Amen!

Sons and Daughters of Our Father in Heaven

Jesus must have endured these kinds of things every day of His life. Why? Because Jesus walked in an incredibly high level of the seer anointing. He always knew the thoughts and intents of people's hearts (Hebrews 4:12). Perhaps that is why He encouraged us to *"love your enemies, bless those who curse you, do good to those who hate you, and pray for those who spitefully use you and persecute you,* **that you may be sons of your Father in heaven**; *for He makes His sun rise on the evil and on the good, and sends rain on the just and on the unjust. For if you love those who love you, what reward have you? Do not even the tax collectors do the same? And if you greet your brethren only, what do you do more than others? Do not even the tax collectors do so? Therefore you shall be perfect, just as your Father in heaven is perfect"* (Matthew 5:44-48, emphasis added).

Search for the Gold

Learn to pray for those who spitefully use you and persecute you, whether it is a local pastor, intercessor, or a witchdoctor in Tanzania. This is a great exercise that can help you to activate a deeper level of the seer anointing in your life! Remember, the seer anointing blossoms in the soil of love! Your discernment will flourish when it is watered by the love of God.

We need to understand that we can have the most powerful healing anointing or revelatory gifts (seer anointing) in our city or nation. However, if our gifting is not motivated by the love of God, our actions can be sinful in the eyes of God. "Shield up!" This is a two-edged sword! When the seer anointing activates in your life, you will be given revelation about the sins and other poor character issues in people's lives. Kathy and I have been experiencing this attribute of the seer anointing for many years. Many times the Lord has given us a vision (seer experience) of people who were working secretly against us or the ministry.

When the Spirit of God opens up this realm, I have stepped into meetings in pastors' offices in other nations (while in my prayer room in America) and listened to conversations. The Lord often allows me to "see" the thoughts and intents of people's hearts. This is not to judge them; this is just an outworking of the seer anointing as it has matured and I have learned to develop my spiritual senses by reason of use.

I have at times stepped into intercessory prayer meetings (while still in my prayer room) to both see and hear what was transpiring and to learn how people were opposing the ministry. There is an example of this sort of discernment in 2 Kings 5:21-27. I have also at times stepped into rooms where witches were involved in occult practices to see and discern their nefarious plans. This kind of revelation is another wonderful dynamic of the seer realm. This kind of seer revelation is a form of the grace of God. These types of seer experiences can be considered some of the hidden mysteries of the seer anointing, in my opinion.

In every single case, such as this, we have found these kinds of seer revelations the Spirit has revealed to us to be extremely accurate. And, in every single case God has supernaturally vindicated us in these situations when we have waited on Him and walked in love. We have learned to stand still and allow God to work on our behalf. Nonetheless, it is still very unpleasant when the Spirit of God gives you real discernment alerting you that people are gossiping, murmuring, complaining, and spreading all manner of lies about you or the church. However, you must stay rooted and grounded in the love of God. Remember, God hates those who sow discord among the brethren. "Ruh roh"; don't do it!

This, too, is an aspect of the seer anointing. You need to understand that when the Lord opens your spiritual eyes and you begin to have the seer anointing activated in your life, you will see and discern both good and evil. You will see the warts, wrinkles, ungodly mindsets, and hidden agendas that many people have. At times you may even discern the idols hidden within other people's hearts. This includes those in the Body of Christ and those involved in the occult. At times like these we must "see" like Christ and we must "be" like Christ (see John 8:11; Luke 23:34).

Learn to see the good in all people (even when they revile and persecute you). We must search for the gold in men's and women's hearts when the seer anointing and discernment reveals to us their sin and shortcomings, even when we know the thoughts and intents of people's hearts are against us. We must remember that the blood of Jesus was shed to cover their shortcomings and sins. We must remember that there is no sin that the blood of Jesus cannot heal. We must remember that even the vilest sinner has a God-ordained DNA and destiny.

We must remember that the Savior is more than capable of transforming their life. Finally, remember, if the Lord reveals these hidden sins and other evil things in people's lives and hearts, He has a purpose for revealing this revelation to you. Perhaps He is showing you these hidden things because you are the one that the Creator of heaven and earth is calling to pray for that person. Perhaps God is calling you to bring them out of darkness and into the marvelous light of the Kingdom of God and into the fullness of His salvation (though you may never speak directly to them or about them).

God reveals things to heal things.

Remember to always SEE the gold in everyone. Purpose in your heart to minister and operate in the seer anointing out of a heart of God's compassion and the founts of the Father's love.

Never judge God's people without God's heart. Otherwise you will pick up the blood that Jesus shed for their healing and salvation. By your unrighteous judgments you will be saying that the blood of Jesus is not able to cleanse them, to heal them, and to save them. You will get the blood of God upon your hands. Trust me in this; you do NOT want the blood of the Lamb on your hands. Always let your discernment flow from the love and compassion of Christ.

In the next chapter we will continue to build on the scriptural foundation that we have laid and study additional keys that can help you understand how the seer anointing operates through the five traditional senses of the human spirit.

CHAPTER 17

The Seer Anointing
and Your Five Traditional Senses

As the seer anointing is activated in your life, you begin to experience things in the spiritual realm. You might see angels or feathers or gold dust. You might hear supernatural singing. You might smell the aroma of God, what some call the "fragrance of the Lord." It is important to note that as exciting and pleasant as these things are, they must not consume our focus and take it away from Jesus. We must stay focused on Him through all of our experiences. We touched on this dynamic of the seer anointing earlier in the book. However, I want to study how discernment works through the five traditional human senses in more detail in this chapter.

It is possible to discern aspects, attributes, and facets from the spiritual realm with all five of your carnal senses. The seer anointing will at times manifest to all of these senses. Scientists recognize the five traditional human senses as sight or vision, hearing, taste, smell, and touch. The seer anointing can work through any one of these senses at a given time and in a given place. However, the seer anointing can vary in how and when it manifests through these traditional senses.

The River of Glory

For example, recently we sponsored a revival meeting in Kansas City where there were an estimated 300 or more people in attendance.

As I stood up to speak, we continued to spontaneously worship the Lord in spirit and in truth. As David Salinas led the worship, I began to decree the seer visions the Spirit was releasing to me in the heavenly realms. At one point the "fragrance of the Lord" filled the sanctuary and an estimated 60 to 70 percent of those in the room were able to smell the supernatural fragrance of roses and cinnamon wafting through the sanctuary. This is an example of a couple of hundred people experiencing the seer realm simultaneously! (This worship event was recorded and is available in our online bookstore. It is called *River of Glory Prophetic Worship*. People have contacted us to testify that they have experienced the same "fragrance of the Lord" as they have listened to this spontaneous worship CD.)

Learning to Operate in the Seer Anointing Can Be a Process

Remember, learning to perceive or activate your seer gift can be a process. It's OK *not* to see into the spiritual realms or to discern supernatural activity the first time out. It's also OK to see something and not understand it, such as a flash of light. Was that or was it not an angel? We learn to grow in our supernatural understanding as we are diligent to exercise our spiritual senses.

The Holy Spirit has been assigned to teach us all things. This is especially true concerning spiritual truths and spiritual phenomena. Since the Holy Spirit releases or imparts the gift of discerning of spirits, as we saw in 1 Corinthians 12:10-11, He can also guide us and teach us all things concerning this spiritual gift. Sometimes we don't fully understand the subtleties of God's gifts to us. For example, with the gift of discerning of spirits, you have to exercise your spiritual senses by reason of use to grow and mature your discernment (Hebrew 5:14). This is how you grow to understand all the idiosyncrasies or the whistles and the bells of the things that God gives us. Sometimes we don't realize what we can do with what God has given us. Growing in maturity in the gifts of God and the seer anointing can be a learning curve, and that is OK too. We need to learn to recognize our power and delegated authority and appropriate who we are "in Christ."

Certificates of Power and Authority

Here is a story that is a good analogy: There was a woman who was a maid to the Queen of England. For eighteen years after she retired, she lived in a shanty and was impoverished. There came a time when she was dying, and a member of her church came to her shanty to bless her. The visitor saw a certificate that was hanging on the wall of the shanty. He asked the woman, "What is this beautiful certificate?" It had a nice seal on it that he recognized as the seal of the Queen. As the visitor read it, he discovered that it was her retirement pension. She was supposed to be living in the palace. The woman was illiterate so she had never read it. As a result, she lived eighteen years in poverty when she should have been living in Buckingham Palace with the royal family.

This is the way it is for some of us spiritually. God, the King, has given us certificates of power and authority that we haven't yet stepped into because we don't understand them—we are spiritually "illiterate." That's true about the seer anointing and the gift of discerning of spirits. Again, we need to remember that learning to step into these things of the Kingdom can be a process. The Lord has given us a Helper to tutor us in the things of the Spirit and to reveal to us His hidden mysteries. We see this role of the Holy Spirit in the following scriptures:

> But when the Helper comes, whom I shall send to you from the Father, the Spirit of truth who proceeds from the Father, He will testify of Me (John 15:26).

> The Holy Spirit, whom the Father will send in My name, He will teach you all things, and bring to your remembrance all things that I said to you (John 14:26).

But the anointing which you have received from Him abides in you, and you do not need that anyone teach you; but as the same anointing teaches you concerning all things, and is true, and is not a lie, and just as it has taught you, you will abide in Him (1 John 2:27).

The Holy Spirit is the giver of the gifts of the Spirit and the gift of discerning of spirits. The anointing comes from Jesus, for He is the anointed One. So when the gifts of the Spirit are poured out upon you, it is really Jesus (each gift demonstrates the character of Christ); it is the nature of Jesus operating through you. When God gives you the gift of discerning of spirits, the anointing abides in you. Again, as we allow the Holy Spirit teach us the things of God and open our spiritual eyes and our spiritual ears and help us to exercise our spiritual senses by reason of use, we can step into the fullness of the rest of God.

We are living in the day and the hour when God wants His people to not just diligently enter into His rest (Hebrews 4:10); He wants us to enter into the *fullness* of His rest. It is in that place where we hear God clearly, we see God clearly, we trust Him, we rest in Him, and we allow His Spirit to teach us all things. Life is no longer a struggle. It is learning to live as mature sons and daughters of God; walking in the seer anointing all the time. It is living in the seer anointing where the grace and favor of God goes before you and makes a way. The seer anointing can release amazing supernatural favor with both God and man. It can activate a supernatural grace to prosper into your life.

People are drawn to the light of your rising. It's no longer about who you are but about who He is in you. The glory of God arises upon you because you are totally sold out to Him and you are allowing His Spirit to pour out through you: "*It is no longer I who live, but Christ lives in me*" (Galatians 2:20). When it is that way, "*Christ in you, the hope of glory*" (Colossians 1:27) pours out through you. The character of Christ pours out through you through the Spirit, through the gifts of the Spirit, and through the anointing of the Holy Spirit.

Warts and Wrinkles

That's the seer anointing, when you are being led by God's Spirit. It's not always about the seeing, hearing, touching, or smelling; it's about having the eyes of your heart activated so that you understand supernatural things and have revelation. You will begin to have God's heart for people.

When our spiritual senses are activated, it's not always going to be pretty. Sometimes God is going to show us the warts and wrinkles on people. If the Lord shows us these things in other people's lives, we can focus on the good and we can speak life and destiny and love into them. God sees the good and wants us to honor what He has put into each person—a seed, spiritual DNA that our Father knit in us before we were put together in our mother's womb. We all have a destiny in God. Again, your destiny is to recreate Christ in your sphere of influence. One of the ways that's going to happen is by having the seer anointing activated in your life so you will be led by God's Spirit continually. The Lord will give you His heart for people like we see outlined in Isaiah 50:4:

> The Lord God has given Me The tongue of the learned, That I should know how to speak A word in season to him who is weary. He awakens Me morning by morning, He awakens My ear To hear as the learned.

As we learn to work in symphony with the Holy Spirit and grow in authority and understanding of Christ's Kingdom, the seer anointing will begin to work within us in a greater and greater measure. God will give you supernatural wisdom and revelation, which are also wonderful attributes of the seer anointing. You will go from one level of grace to another level grace and power in the seer anointing. You will move from glory to glory in the Kingdom. You will supernaturally develop amazing favor with both God and man.

In the next chapter we will look at additional scriptural keys that can help you understand how the seer anointing can help you grow in favor with both God and man. This revelation can make easier for you to unlock the hidden mystery of the seer anointing in your life.

CHAPTER 18

Wisdom to Grow in
Favor with God and Man

The Lord wants to awaken our spirit. The Spirit of God wishes to release a revival in our lives that is activated through our spirit. He wants to awaken us morning by morning. He wishes to open our ears to spiritual truths and awaken our ears to hear as the learned (Isaiah 50:4). How do the learned listen and hear? They hear with revelation and heavenly understanding, which enable them to comprehend and perceive heavenly truth. The Father wants for you and me to know the mysteries and secrets of His Kingdom, for it is the Father's good pleasure to give us the Kingdom (Luke 8:18; 12:32).

God wants for us to see and hear amazing revelatory knowledge from the hidden depths of the heavenly realms. We can learn the mysteries of the Kingdom of God when we are diligent to walk in intimacy and communion with the Lord. We can learn the mysteries of the Kingdom of God when we walk close to Jesus. When we come into that place, God can give us wisdom and we can grow in favor with both God and man. This is another blessing of the seer anointing.

We need only to ask God for the wisdom we need (Colossians 1:9-10; James 1:5). Scripture clearly illustrates this concept. We have privileges and open invitations to ask the Lord to give us spiritual understanding. We can ask the Lord to activate the eyes of our spirit, the eyes of our heart, our spiritual eyes. God will activate the seer anointing within us. We learned in Genesis 1 that God was a seer and that we were created in His image. We are to be seers as He is. As we have learned "seeing" is more than just hearing or seeing in the spirit; it is having a total revelation of everything that is happening around you—not only in the natural but also in the spiritual realms. Jesus taught about these hidden mysteries of the seer anointing in Luke 8.

> *And He* [Jesus] *said, "To you it has been given to know the mysteries of the Kingdom of God, but to the rest it is given in parables, that 'seeing they may not see, And hearing they may not understand'"* (Luke 8:10).

I believe that you can have a supernatural grace come upon your life like the boy Samuel. Remember, Samuel was a seer and a man of favor: *"The child Samuel grew in stature, and in favor both with the Lord and men"* (1 Samuel 2:26). It is one thing to be saved; but it is another thing to have the great grace, supernatural blessings, and favor of God evident upon your life. The seer anointing can help you to grow into that place of favor with both God and man. Everything that you do will prosper. Everything that you set your hands to will be fruitful and multiply. You will walk in an unusual level of revelation, and the power and gifting of the Holy Spirit will be evident in your sphere of influence.

People will be drawn to the glory of the Lord that will be seen upon you (Isaiah 60). When you begin to experience the seer realm with all five of your physical senses, there will be times or places where you will discover and discern a porous spot in the spiritual realm. At times and at places like this, your gift to see will be activated in a greater degree. I call places like these a Mahanaim; a geographical place where the spirit realm is easily accessible. In this place you will begin to see and hear and taste and touch and discern and understand revelatory things from the Kingdom of God.

I am referring to understanding and comprehending the attributes or facts concerning the realm of the spirit. We also have a wonderful invitation to seek God for help, understanding, and spiritual wisdom. Scripture is full of promises, such as the following:

For this reason we also, since the day we heard it, do not cease to pray for you, and to ask that you may be filled with the knowledge of His will in all wisdom and spiritual understanding; that you may walk worthy of the Lord, fully pleasing Him, being fruitful in every good work and increasing in the knowledge of God (Colossians 1:9-10).

As we touched on earlier, you can begin to experience the seer realm by all five of your physical senses at various times and places. This comes through entertaining and exercising our inherent spiritual gifting to see. Ask God for this, seek Him diligently, and ask Him for His spiritual understanding (Matthew 7:7). The Kingdom is the ability to understand the gift of the discerning of spirits, to step into that, to operate in the seer anointing, to have it activated in your life, and to impact your sphere of influence for God's glory. By being diligent to learn to see, you will also be learning how to become a carrier of God's tangible glory and the Kingdom of Heaven. Having such supernatural wisdom and understanding is pleasing to the Lord.

In the beginning of this book, I shared my testimony about how I began to press into the Kingdom of God and how I asked the Lord to increase my ability to see the spiritual realm that I perceived as a new believer. I began to exercise my spiritual senses by reason of use. When I began to massage my spiritual senses, the Spirit of God helped me to understand principles concerning the seer anointing. My ability to see into the spirit has greatly increased during the last decade through this ongoing process of exercising my spiritual senses.

You can also begin to exercise your spiritual senses and your seer gifting in a similar way. Let's take some time to elaborate on this dynamic in more detail.

It is also important to remember that seer experiences can transpire in your dreams. There are hundreds of ways that the Lord can open up the heavens to you and allow you to interact with His Kingdom and activate the seer anointing in your life. You need not be concerned, focused, or fixated with any one method. However, it is possible that the most important way to exercise and activate your seer gifting is simply to ask. Let's do that now. In fact, I want to encourage you to pray all of the prayers in this book frequently. Don't just read them once. I recommend that you copy them and pray the prayers of activation and healing that are in this book frequently. Pray them daily. This will help you grow in favor with both God and man.

Prayer of Activation

Lord, Your word promises me that if I ask, it will be given to me; if I seek, I will find; and when I knock, You will open a hidden mystery to me. Father, in James 1:5 You promised me that if I lack wisdom, to ask of You, who gives to everyone liberally and without reproach, and it will be given to me. Today, Lord, in the mighty name of Jesus Christ of Nazareth, I ask You to release to me heavenly wisdom and revelation liberally and without any reproach. Lord, I ask that You would help me to learn to minister and live in the glory realms and that You would activate the seer anointing in my life. Lord, I ask that You would give me wisdom and revelation and a Christ-like character that will help me to walk in nobility and humility. Lord, release supernatural help to me as I learn to grow in godly discernment. Lord, activate my supernatural DNA and ability to see into the spiritual realms of the Kingdom of God. Father, I thank You for unlocking and giving to me knowledge of the hidden mysteries of the Kingdom of God. In Jesus name I pray. Amen.

In the next chapter we will continue to look at the idiosyncrasies of the Kingdom of God and learn additional scriptural keys that can help us unlock the hidden mysteries of the seer anointing in our lives.

CHAPTER 19

Apostolic Prayers
and Your Spiritual Senses

If you study of the prayers of the Apostle Paul, you will find that he always prays about the good things God was doing in lives. Paul always searched for the gold in people and in the Body of Christ. Even when the church was embroiled in sin, Paul always started his epistles by recognizing and honoring the good things that were in the church he was addressing. That is an important lesson for us to remember as seers. The following prayer for the Ephesian church is a good example of this. I encourage you to pray this apostolic prayer of Paul over your life every day.

[I] do not cease to give thanks for you, making mention of you in my prayers: that the God of our Lord Jesus Christ, the Father of glory, may give to you the spirit of wisdom and revelation [the seer anointing] *in the knowledge of Him,* **the eyes of your understanding being enlightened**; *that you may know what is the hope of His calling, what are the riches of the glory of His inheritance in the saints* [we are the saints; the inheritance is in us], *and what is the exceeding greatness of His power toward us who believe, according to the working of His mighty power which He worked in Christ when He raised Him from the dead and seated Him at His right hand in the heavenly places* [glory realms], *far above all principality and power and might and dominion, and every name that is named, not only in this age but also in that which is to come. And He put all things under His feet, and gave Him to*

*be head over all things to the church, which is His body, **the fullness of Him** who fills all in all* (Ephesians 1:16-23, emphasis added).

This is an apostolic prayer. Paul prays for the eyes of your understanding "to be enlightened"; it means to shed light upon or to reveal clearly. We all have a "knowing" released to us by the Holy Spirit. This supernatural knowledge could be also defined as the gift of discerning of spirits or the seer anointing. This anointing of the seer realm will often work in symphony with the unction of the Holy Spirit as we have studied earlier.

When Paul prays for the "eyes" of your understanding, he is not referring to our natural eyes or eyesight. Paul is referring to the eye of the soul or spirit or our supernatural vision. The word translated "understanding" in this passage is the Greek word *kardias*, literally "heart." Paul's intention here is not the physical heart but the place of consciousness, self-awareness, or understanding; such as knowing, believing, or loving with "all of your heart." This "understanding" can also mean supernatural thought or mind, or to have the mind of God or the mind of the Spirit of God, and/or to have or experience the mind of Christ.

Paul desired for people to understand that we have a spiritual inheritance and spiritual nature that we can step into. We need to understand our true nature in Christ. We have the mind of Christ (1 Corinthians 2:16). When the eyes of our understanding are opened, we begin to appreciate and comprehend who we really are in Christ Jesus. When the eyes of our understanding are activated, we can begin to see and enter into the Kingdom of Heaven. When we begin to enter into the realms of heaven, we can begin to appropriate the power and authority that is our heavenly inheritance.

When Jesus Christ's body was lying in a grave, His spirit was busy. He plundered hell and took back the keys of death and Hades (see Ephesians 4:9; Revelation 1:18). He gave them to us; He has given us the keys to the Kingdom (Matthew 16:18-19). He has given us power and authority. As the seer anointing is activated in our lives, we can rise up above demonic powers and principalities and learn to live in the glory realms. From that place there is no warfare; from that place we receive revelation; from the glory we receive divine power to overcome the enemy and to live in total victory in Christ. This is another anointing and level of the seer anointing. We become seated with Christ in the heavenly places (Ephesians 1:3; 2:6).

Our spiritual senses allow us to be transformed into the likeness of Christ Jesus and activated into the seer anointing just like Jesus (John 14:12). Remember, Jesus was a seer.

Experience the Spiritual Realms

As our spiritual senses are opened, we will begin to experience things in the spirit realm. On numerous occasions the Lord has opened my spiritual eyes or the eyes of my heart and I have seen demonic spirits of infirmity. I have seen one spirit of infirmity that is associated with the flu. It looks like a combination of a Chihuahua dog, a bat, and a monkey. I have seen this spirit of infirmity clinging onto many sick people. When I command that devil to loose the person in the name of Jesus, the demon jumps off of their back and scampers away, whimpering as it goes. Other spirits of infirmity look like various types of serpents. These can be associated with chronic headaches, breathing problems, body pain, and especially back problems. Again, when you see these spirits of infirmity, you have all authority over them. The Lord first began to show these things to me in 2001 to help equip me to release healing in Africa to His people there.

Once I was in Tanzania on a missions trip with forty other people. Twenty-three of them got flu-like symptoms. We were having a prayer meeting one morning when my spiritual eyes opened. (This was right after Jesus visited me on the Sea of Glass like Crystal and told me to begin to study the seer anointing.) I saw these bat-like demonic beings hanging onto people. I said, "Wow, what is that, Lord?" He said, "That's the flu. Break it off of them." So I started praying for people. I took my spiritual sword out and cut these demons of infirmity off with my spiritual sword. Most of the twenty-three were instantly healed. The weapons of our warfare are mighty through God!

Remember, Jesus told us,

*The Son can do nothing of Himself, but what He **sees** the Father do; for whatever He does, the Son also does in like manner* (John 5:19, emphasis added).

Our spiritual senses enable us to step into the spirit or heavenly places where our supernatural inheritance is waiting for us. Again, it is my opinion that Jesus saw into the demonic realm the way that I have just described. Spiritual senses or the seer anointing are an element of our very being. We are creatures created by God in His image with a spirit, soul, and body. We are created in God's very image to "see." You are created to live and breathe in the seer anointing.

Our five physical senses are the operation of our body, flesh, or carnal self. The eyes of our understanding, or spiritual senses, are the part of our spirit that can also comprehend things that are present in the spiritual realm in a similar fashion that our eyes, ears, nose, skin, and tongue perceive elements and phenomenon from the natural realm. Spiritual senses operate in the spiritual realm in a similar way that our five carnal senses detect elements in the natural realm. Our spiritual senses perceive elements and phenomenon from the spirit.

There are other types of demonic devices that you will be able to perceive when the gift of discerning of spirits is activated in your life. At times you will see the enemy's weapons of warfare. I have on many occasions seen arrows, chains, knives, shackles, or darts that have pierced a person suffering from a number of debilitating conditions. When you remove the demonic weapons, these people are almost always immediately made whole.

This is an area of the seer anointing that we can all grow and mature into. In the next chapter we will continue to look at some more idiosyncrasies and scriptural keys that can help us to learn how to unlock additional hidden mysteries of the seer anointing.

CHAPTER 20

Entering into the Spirit and Heavenly Places

When the eyes of our understanding, or spiritual senses, are activated, we are beginning to experience life through our spirit. As we have learned, that part of our being becomes dominant in terms of perception. This can last for a few seconds or it can last for days, as we learn how to walk in the spirit. This can be the outworking of the gift of discerning of spirits activating in our life or what can be considered our spiritual senses. Spiritual understanding can at times also be the gifts of prophecy, the word of knowledge, and the word of wisdom manifesting in our life. Let's look at this dynamic of the seer anointing in more detail.

In Enoch's life this walk was eternal. *"Enoch walked with God; and he was not, for God took him"* (Genesis 5:24). That is what I want!

In 2 Kings 2:11 it tells us what happened to Elijah: *"Then it happened, as they continued on and talked, that suddenly a chariot of fire appeared with horses of fire, and separated the two of them; and Elijah went up by a whirlwind into heaven."*

Jesus' experience is outlined in Acts 1:9: *"Now when He had spoken these things, while they watched, He was taken up, and a cloud received Him out of their sight."*

Is it possible to have seer experiences like Enoch, Elijah, and Jesus today? I believe *you can*. We, too, have the liberty to enter into heavenly places. How are we going to get there? We get there by getting our seer anointing activated; by getting our ability to hear activated; by getting the unction of the Holy Spirit flowing through us; by submitting to the refining fire of the Holy Spirit and allowing that process of sanctification to work in our lives; by stepping on that Highway of Holiness mentioned in Isaiah 35:8; and by allowing the Holy Spirit to sanctify us and purify us so that our vessel is prepared to receive the gifts that God has for us. I write about this dynamic in my book *Unlocking the Mysteries of the Powers of the Age to Come.*

Remember God Is a Spirit

Jesus put it this way: *"The hour is coming, and now is, when the true worshipers will worship the Father in spirit and truth; for the Father is seeking such to worship Him. God is Spirit, and those who worship Him must worship in spirit and truth"* (John 4:23-24).

The word translated "Spirit" in this passage is the Greek word *pneuma.* "Worship" comes from the Greek word that also means "kiss." In a sense, this language indicates the Lord wants us to kiss Him in the spiritual realm the way a faithful dog licks his loving master. We are welcome and have standing invitations to access the spiritual realm where God's Kingdom exists. We can enter that place without "trespassing" because of the finished work of Calvary and the precious blood of the Lamb of God. The Cross of Calvary is the most important key and *only* bridge to legitimate seer experiences.

"If then you were raised with Christ, seek those things which are above, where Christ is, sitting at the right hand of God. Set your mind on things above, not on things on the earth. For you died, and your life [everything about you—your mind, your will, your emotions, your aspirations, your ministry, your children, your family, your home, your car, your money] *is hidden with Christ in God"* (Colossians 3:1-3). That is where Enoch and Elijah are now; they are hidden with Christ in God! Jesus is in the Secret Place of the Most High God, but He is also hidden within our hearts. Amazing, isn't it!

I believe that we all have been given the liberty and privilege to pass through the heavens. The question becomes, do we believe it and do we receive it? This is an individual choice that each one of us must make. The Lord gives each of us the liberty to have as little or as much of His Kingdom as we desire. Question for you: how hungry are you for the Kingdom of Heaven?

[God] *raised us up together, and made us sit together in the heavenly places in Christ Jesus, that in the ages to come He might show the exceeding riches of His grace in His kindness toward us in Christ Jesus* (Ephesians 2:6-7).

Discovering the Seer Anointing

At times the Holy Spirit in us can alert us to the supernatural or spiritual activity around us. This is the activation of the seer anointing. Discovering the seer anointing is much more that just seeing into the spiritual realm—sometimes you can smell it or sense it. Other times you just have a "knowing," which we have learned is the unction of the Holy Spirit, another element of the seer realm.

Some of the most powerful releases of angelic encounters and seer experiences that I've experienced have not been when I've seen the angels (and I do see them) but when I've just known that the seer realm is unfolding around me. When the seer anointing gives you revelation that God's angels are present, it is a good idea to speak to the Holy Spirit asking Him why the Lord has sent His angels. Most of the time when the Lord sends His angels into your sphere of influence, there is a grace for you to co-labor with them to release the ministry that God has ordained for them to accomplish.

Sometimes in the seer realm you work in unity with the Holy Spirit to activate God's angels to release miracles and healing. At other times God may send His angels to release signs and wonders. Perhaps heavenly angels can be released into your life and ministry to manifest supernatural provision. (For a more teaching on this aspect of the seer anointing and learning to co-labor with God's angels, we recommend that you get the teaching series, *Cultivating the Glory 3 DVD School*.)

I welcome these kinds of supernatural phenomenon. Remember, the seer anointing is also a means that God can activate to alert us to the presence and activity of the demonic realm. As I wrote, I personally call this aspect of the seer anointing the "Astro anointing," "Ruh roh." Our spiritual senses are, on occasion, an extension of the gift of discerning of spirits and/or the revelatory gifts of the Holy Spirit.

When we operate in the seer anointing, we will begin to work in symphony with the Holy Spirit that dwells within us. Nonetheless, we can still employ Paul's apostolic prayer (Ephesians 1:16-23) to activate the eyes of our understanding (hearts) and the seer gifting in our lives. Pray that prayer over your life on a daily basis, asking the Lord to activate the seer anointing in your life. We can biblically seek to increase our ability to perceive the supernatural activity in the spiritual realm that is all around us.

Paranoid of the Paranormal

Understanding how our spiritual senses operate in relationship to the supernatural should not be a fearful idea or proposition. God is a Spirit. He dwells in a spiritual Kingdom. If you hope to enter into heaven, you are striving to enter God's supernatural and spiritual home. The reality is that the spiritual Kingdom of Heaven is all around you at this second.

The realm of the spirit, where Jesus Christ is seated at the right hand of the Father (Colossians 3:1), is more real than the book in your hands right now. The ability to enter into this spiritual Kingdom and realm of the spirit should be normal for us too. That is what the seer anointing is all about. This spiritual gift will help you to appropriate your inheritance as a joint heir with Christ.

However, many in the Body of Christ have allowed the world to "steal" their spiritual heritage—the supernatural—which has now become "too spooky and mystical" for most people. The opposite should be true. We should be at home in the supernatural realm where our God dwells. You should not be paranoid of the paranormal.

We all have a spiritual inheritance and spiritual nature that we can step into and activate. The Lord will begin to accelerate this process in the coming season. Ordinary people will access the Kingdom of Heaven and start to exercise their spiritual senses by reason of use. They will surely begin to experience the supernatural elements of God's Kingdom.

More and more ordinary people are beginning to walk in the seer anointing. Occasionally this will include encounters with angels. As the seer anointing becomes more common in your life, you will begin to overcome the fear of the unknown. You will have supernatural encounters and operate in the seer anointing on a regular basis.

Prayer to Activate Your Spiritual Destiny

Lord, I pray that we would begin to see like Jesus; that the anointing to see would be activated in our lives. I pray, Father, that You would increase that gift to see already upon many of us and that you would activate it for those who have a dormant gift. Lord, I ask for the stirring up of the gifts of the Spirit. I ask for the release of the gift of the discerning of spirits. Lord, I ask for the unction of the Holy Spirit to come upon us. I ask that You would give us wisdom and revelation and that You would show us anything that is hindering us from walking in the fullness of everything You've taught us to do. I pray that our spirit man would become dominant in our lives and that the eyes of our understanding would become activated. I thank You for activation; I thank You that You are releasing gifts. Here we are; we are Your children, and we are for signs and wonders from the Lord of Hosts. I pray in Jesus' mighty name.

Lay your hand on your heart and say, *"Jesus, I ask You to open up the eyes of my understanding. Enlighten my heart. Prepare me to step into this realm. Help me to understand what Your word says—not what I think Your word says, not what I've been taught Your word says, but what Your word really says about my ability to see. Lord, I ask that You would activate the gift of discerning of spirits in my life. And with it, Lord, I ask for wisdom; I ask that You would release to me the spirit of wisdom and revelation. And right now, Father, I promise to give You all the praise, all the honor, and all the glory for the magnificent, supernatural miracles, healings, and signs and wonders that You are going to do through me. In Jesus' might name I pray. Amen."*

In the next chapter we will study the apostolic prayers of Jesus that can supernaturally open the heavens over your life.

CHAPTER 21

The Seer Anointing and Open Heavens

In Luke 3 we see an amazing seer experience unfold. We see Jesus beginning His ministry. One of the first things that happens is that as Jesus submits to the ministry of John the Baptist and He prays. The Holy Spirit comes upon Him and the heavens open up over His life. When we examine the life of Jesus Christ, we see that Jesus walked in an extremely high level of supernatural activity. Jesus' life was punctuated with an abundance of supernatural events. He operated in the seer anointing. Jesus was a seer. There were a lot of angelic visitations and a lot of supernatural things that happened in the Lord's life while He walked upon the earth. There were many instances we see in Scripture of the seer anointing operating in the life of the Messiah. This fact begs the question, why and how did that happen? The scripture in Luke 3 demonstrates that Christ walked under an open heaven.

> *When all the people were baptized, it came to pass that Jesus also was baptized; and while He prayed, the heaven was opened. And the Holy Spirit descended in bodily form like a dove upon Him, and a voice came from heaven which said, "You are My beloved Son; in You I am well pleased"* (Luke 3:21-22).

So, if Jesus walked in such a high level of signs and wonders and He has called us to walk in that same level of signs and wonders and to do even greater works, how are we going to do that? One of the ways is that we are only going to do those things that Jesus is doing. Jesus said in John 5:19, *"The Son...can do only what he sees his Father doing"* (NIV). Jesus did not start His ministry until the heavens were opened over His life. That fact is very important.

Chapters 2 and 4 in the Book of Hebrews, as well as other passages, clearly demonstrate that Jesus was a man with a nature just like ours. I encourage you to search out this nature of Jesus yourself. He was God but He was also a human being just like us. Christ was divine, but He was also fully man.

So how can we explain the abundance of supernatural activity and the wealth of the seer anointing operating in the Lord's earthly life? How did He get translated across the Sea of Galilee? How did He multiply the bread? How did He raise the dead? How did Jesus do all of those incredible miracles, signs, and wonders if He had a human nature like us? One answer to this question is found in Luke 3:21-22: *"And while He prayed, the heaven was opened. And the Holy Spirit descended in bodily form like a dove upon Him."*

Jesus Has the Freedom to Enter into the Heavens

What a powerful portrait of the love of the Father and the freedom that Christ had to enter into the realms of heaven! Others were also drawn into the open heaven because the ears and eyes of their understanding were activated so they could hear Papa God speak and they could see the Holy Spirit descend in the bodily form of a dove. So the seer anointing was in operation. This incident in Luke 3 marks the first time that all three parts of the Godhead were together in unity upon the earth since creation or the Garden of Eden. Therefore, this event has an important and substantial parabolic significance.

In Eden Adam and Eve walked under an open heaven on a continuous basis with no interruption in their communion with the Godhead. The Bible doesn't tell us how long this open heaven in Eden lasted, but it could have been thousands of years. Can you imagine how wonderful it would have been to walk in constant communion with God? They saw God clearly. They heard God clearly all the time.

We can have this wonderful kind of relationship with the Lord today. It is our spiritual destiny; it's in our spiritual DNA to walk and talk and have communion with God. We need to remember that this ability is a gift of grace given to all freely through the finished work of Jesus Christ on the Cross of Calvary. Remember, the Cross is the key to open heavens. The Cross of Calvary is a key that can unlock the mysteries of the seer anointing in your life.

This was one of the primary missions of the Messiah. Jesus came to earth to secure our salvation and to give us a supernatural inheritance. Part of that inheritance was that He came to open up the heavens over mankind. The heavens were brass over our heads, and we did not have the liberty to have communion and intimacy with God. When Jesus prayed and the heavens open on that day in Luke 3, He restored something to us which is basic in our relationship with the Lord. We need to go beyond our salvation to intimacy with God. God is raising up mature sons and daughters who can see and hear and touch and taste and smell things in the spiritual realms—those who can interact with God's Kingdom.

Luke 17 tells us, *"The kingdom of God is within you"* (v. 21). So, by the grace of God, when we are saved our spirit man becomes alive and our spiritual DNA given to us by Papa God becomes activated. I personally believe that the moment you pray to receive Jesus Christ as Savior, every single spiritual gift that is in 1 Corinthians 12 is activated in your life. I believe that anyone can minister in any gifts of the Holy Spirit. I also believe that you can operate in any of the five offices found in Ephesians 4. I believe that anytime, anywhere the Holy Spirit can well up within you and if God needs you to minister in any particular anointing, you can do it. This doesn't mean you necessarily sit in these ministry offices (pastor, prophet, teacher, evangelist, or apostle) but that any of these anointings can flow through you at any time as the Holy Spirit wills. (This is my opinion and may not agree with some theology.) "Ruh roh"!

Enter the Presence Behind the Veil

This hope we have as an anchor of the soul, both sure and steadfast, and which enters the Presence behind the veil, where the forerunner has entered for us, even Jesus, having become High Priest forever according to the order of Melchizedek (Hebrews 6:19-20).

Jesus is the forerunner. A forerunner is someone who blazes a trail for other people to follow. Jesus blazed a trail into heavenly realms for each of us to follow. One of the ways He did that was by reinstating our heritage as human beings to have open heavens over our lives. When the heavens are opened over our lives, we can step into the spiritual realms (behind the veil) and we can begin to hear, see, smell, taste, touch, and have the eyes of our spirit activated to discern things in the spiritual realm. This is another aspect of the seer anointing.

To experience open heavens is only possible because of the mission of the Messiah. When He prayed in Luke 3, He restored open heavens to mankind; that's why we can step into it and operate in the seer anointing. If it wasn't for the finished work of Jesus on the Cross, we could not receive the seer anointing to become royal priests forever according to the order of Melchizedek. And this position is what gives us the authority to enter the heavenly realms. The seer anointing is part of the mantle or anointing of Melchizedek. It is one of the five levels of the rest of the Lord. I suggest that you read my book *The Sword of the Lord, and the Rest of the Lord* for more revelation on this dynamic of the mantle of Melchizedek and the seer anointing.

Sowing into the Glory

It is also true that if you want to have a particular ministry gift activated in your life, you should find a ministry that operates in the gift you are seeking and then submit to the authority of that ministry. Go to their meetings, sit under their anointing, pray for them, sow financially into their ministry, and help that ministry as the Spirit of the Lord leads you. When you become an armor bearer and serve a ministry, the anointing that's on that ministry comes upon you. A spiritual key is to submit to their authority. In the spiritual realm if you do not submit to authority, you will not have authority. A good biblical example of all of this would be Elijah and Elisha found in 2 Kings 2. (For more detailed teaching on this subject get my DVD teaching *Sowing into the Glory*.)

You can also accelerate your seer gifting when you learn to rip or rend the heavens over your life. In the next chapter we will look at several scriptural keys that can help you understand how you can open the heavens over your life and sphere of influence. Learn to take the Kingdom by force (Matthew 11:12). However, we must remember that the Lord is the one responsible for opening the heavens and releasing the seer anointing today.

CHAPTER 22

God Still Opens the Heavens

When Jesus prayed on the day that He was baptized, the heavens opened up over His life. The result was that Christ began His ministry under an open heaven and operated under an open heaven from that day forward. By walking under an open heaven, you can have the seer anointing multiply in your life and ministry too. You may receive the seer anointing by reading this book and praying the prayers of activation in it. Or, you may need to do as Elisha did and smite the waters (see 2 Kings 2:14). You need to keep on banging, keep on asking, keep on knocking, keep on believing God to give you supernatural experiences. Press in until you get your breakthrough.

So we understand that there was a God-ordained moment of time that the Father predetermined to open the heavens over Jesus and consequently reopened the heavens over His creation, mankind. This was the beginning of ministry in Christ's life.

Jesus benefited from the open heavens over His life throughout His earthly ministry. One of the benefits of walking under an open heaven is the ability to see and hear clearly from the spiritual realms. It was the open heavens that Jesus ministered under that helped prepare Him and also empower Him to see and hear clearly what the Father was instructing Him to do. The seer anointing helped the Lord manifest the Kingdom of God at various times and places in His earthly life. Walking under an open heaven is one of the benefits of activating the seer anointing in your life. And these blessings are also what we are defining as the seer anointing.

We need to understand that God is the one who is responsible for opening the heavens over our lives today. This is the sovereign work of the Holy Spirit. It tells us in Luke 3 that God took Jesus to a specific place at a specific time under the ministry of a specific man and then Jesus did a specific act. God is a chronological God.

We need to remember that Jesus is our role model and that He has given us an example to follow. (See John 13:15; Philippians 2:5; 1 Peter 2:21; 1 John 2:6.) Jesus came to earth to break open the heavenly realm for us all. That was a critical aspect of Christ's call and mission. He came to give each of us power and authority. Remember, the enemy doesn't want us to see, hear, taste, smell, or touch the heavenly realms or to have revelatory knowledge from the Kingdom of Heaven. He wants to keep us spiritually deaf, dumb, and blind. Sometimes he puts spiritual blinders over our eyes or sticks demonic plugs in our ears. We can break those things off with our spiritual weapons of warfare (2 Corinthians 10:4).

Living Under an Open Heaven

Living under an open heaven is not only possible but it is imperative. One benefit of living under an open heaven is the activation of the seer anointing in your life and in your sphere of influence. Continue to press in and ask God to activate the eyes of your understanding and your spiritual senses. Ask God to open or rend the heavens over you so that you can begin to function in the seer realm. One of the most important things that Jesus gave you and me the delegated authority to do was to open the heavens over our lives and over our spheres of influence. In Acts 1:8 Jesus told His disciples to go into Judea and Samaria—the places that were in their sphere of influence—and then to ends of the earth. That's what He wants us to do today. God will open up the heavens over your life according to the sphere of your influence—your own family first, then to your city. If you are obedient in these first things, He will expand your sphere of influence beyond that, even to the ends of the earth. When you walk under an open heaven, it goes with you wherever you go.

Why is that important? So that we can see and hear clearly from the heavenly realms; so that we can live with perfect discernment and operate in the seer anointing. You see, when you begin to mature and grow in your ability to operate and minister in the seer anointing, your life and ministry will be transformed. You will begin to demonstrate the Kingdom of God the way Jesus did, with demonstrations of the power of God. Miracles signs and wonders will follow you because the heavens will be open over your life.

The Most Crucial Keys to Opening the Heavens— Prayer and Repentance

We all need to repent. We are humans in this imperfect world, so we all sin and fall short of God's glory (see Romans 3:23). In 1 John 1:9 we read, "*If we confess our sins, He is faithful and just to forgive us our sins and to cleanse us from all unrighteousness.*" God not only forgives us, but He cleanses us. This is so important, because if we are not cleansed, the Holy Spirit won't stay. Receive your cleansing from God to purify your vessel, to burn out those things that keep you from receiving the fullness of God's anointing.

I would encourage you to walk in repentance as a lifestyle; I do. My wife and I practice Communion each day. When we sit and seek the Lord together in this way, His presence comes. As we partake of Communion on the porch of our cabin in Moravian Falls, we have a pair of bluebirds that come and perch on a bird house that I built and they sing to us. If we live a lifestyle of communion, we can draw close to God, and He will draw closer to us.

In Luke 3:21-22 we learned some important keys to opening the heavens. Let's examine them in more detail. We see that the heavens opened over Jesus as He submitted to the ministry of John the Baptist and was baptized and while He prayed. He modeled repentance for us. Therefore, we should also seek to be baptized and to also to pray like Christ. Baptism is symbolic of repentance of sin. Of course, Jesus had no sin. He was the Lamb without spot or blemish (1 Peter 1:19); but He was also our role model and He has given us an example to follow.

The Scriptures do not tell us what kind of prayer that Jesus prayed as He was baptized. However, I am certain that He prayed for the heavens to be opened. This is perhaps the most important key to opening the heavens over your life—prayer. Jesus gave us the authority to ask the Father for open heavens in His name. (See John 16:23.) I do this frequently, praying and asking the Lord to open the heavens over my life and the ministry.

We also see that Jesus began His ministry after the heavens opened over His life. When the heavens opened over the Lord, we see that there was immediate fruit or manifestations of God's Kingdom. The first thing that is apparent in the open heaven over Christ's life is the visible manifestation of the Holy Spirit descending in the bodily form of a dove. This is a demonstration of the seer anointing. Miracles, signs, and wonders abounded in the open heaven that manifested over Jesus that day. What is really being described in this passage is that the corporate anointing to see into the spiritual realm was released and people saw the Holy Spirit manifest in a tangible form as a dove.

Actually, when the heavens opened over Jesus, the gift of discerning of spirits or the seer anointing was activated. Everyone who was in the proximity of Jesus stepped into that open heaven and began to hear and see into the spiritual realm. The people had their spiritual eyes opened to see the dove and their ears opened to hear the Father speak in an audible voice, saying, *"You are My beloved Son, in whom I am well pleased"* (Mark 1:11). This is the fruit of an open heaven; hearing God well.

Remember the seer anointing can be more than just seeing in the spirit. You will note that the Father was speaking to Jesus. But because of the open heaven that was over Christ at that moment, many of the people present both saw and heard into and from the spiritual realm. They entered into the spirit by proximity. They heard God and they saw God, just like in the Garden of Eden. The seer anointing was released en masse to those present that day. And I believe that the seer anointing is being released en masse to those today who have their hearts turned towards the Lord.

And that is why it is absolutely necessary that each of us seek to open the heavens over our lives and activate the seer gifting within us. We need to *hear* God clearly. We need to *see* what God is doing clearly. These two things are imperative, and we can accomplish them in a much more effective way when we get the heavens open over our lives. There is a purpose beyond our pleasure of seeing and hearing things in the spirit realm. God is activating the seer anointing so that we can co-labor with His Spirit and His Kingdom to accomplish what He wants done—healing, deliverance, etc.

I want to encourage you that we are receiving many wonderful testimonies of people who have read the books and testimonies from my trilogy, *The Reality of Angelic Ministry Today*, who are beginning to experience the effects of open heavens. They are starting to have the seer anointing activated in their lives and perceive things from the spiritual realm, including angelic activity. And they are also learning that they can work or co-labor with God's angels. (You can find the trilogy of books and the *School of Angelic Ministry* DVD or CD teaching series on our website bookstore.)

It is also important to remember that we can still enter into or access the open heavens today by proximity just like the disciples and the other people who were present at the River Jordan that day. When Jesus prayed, the people had their spiritual senses activated. They saw into the heavenly realms they heard the supernatural voice of the Father. Anointed prayers can still open the heavens. You can also get the heavens opened and activate your seer gift by going to a geographical place where the heavens are already open. You can also activate the seer anointing by investing time with an individual or ministry that lives and operates under an open heaven. In the next chapter we will continue to study more scriptural keys that can help you enter into an open heaven by proximity. God can help you learn personal secrets and give you keys that can help you unlock the mysteries of the seer anointing in your life when you experience an open heaven.

CHAPTER 23

Entering into Open Heavens and the Seer Anointing by Proximity

As we learned in the last chapter, Peter, James, and John were present and witnessed this supernatural event at the River Jordan when the heavens opened over the life of Jesus (Luke 3). They also witnessed the fruit of the open heaven that was continuously over Jesus. On several other occasions they entered into the spiritual realms by being in proximity to the open heaven that was upon the Lord as they walked with Jesus.

These men told the religious leaders who had crucified Jesus (and who could well have crucified them) this: *"For we cannot but speak the things which we have seen and heard"* (Acts 4:20). What are they talking about? At the Jordan River they heard the voice of the Father and saw the Holy Spirit in the form of a dove. On the Mount of Transfiguration, they saw Moses and Elijah and they clearly heard Father God speak directly to them as individuals. In the upper room of Acts 2, the Holy Spirit actually came upon them in great power, which also came with great grace. They had grace to step into the seer anointing; and as they saw what God was doing, they began to work miracles. The apostles received an impartation from the Lord, and they operated in a very high level of the seer anointing.

It is important that we understand that there are certain characteristics of an open heaven that we can still benefit from today. Primarily these include the seer anointing or the ability to recognize heavenly things and also to both see and hear from the heavenly realms or the spiritual dimensions (plural). (See Genesis 1:1; 2:4; Isaiah 42:5; 45:12-18; Ephesians 1:3, 20; 2:6; 3:10; 6:12.)

Both of these benefits are absolutely critical if we are to fulfill the mandate of Matthew 6:10 and pray like Jesus prays: *"Your kingdom come. Your will be done On earth as it is in heaven."*

The Supernatural Unction of the Holy Spirit

As we learned previously we can also experience the supernatural unction of the Holy Spirit when we live under open heavens (1 John 2:20, KJV). The unction of the Holy Spirit is a characteristic or a part of the seer anointing. This unction may look different with different people because each of us is different and God always speaks to and through us in our own individual language. Your seer anointing will be a personalized thing.

Open heavens will increase the level of the seer anointing in our lives. As a result the ability to see, hear, and to receive, supernatural revelations from the Kingdom of Heaven will greatly increase in your life. We need all of these in the hour in which we live. Of course, the gifting to "see" or the seer anointing is one of the fruits of living under an open heaven.

When the heavens opened over Jesus, the people present saw and heard into the spirit realm. These were ordinary people who saw into and heard from the spiritual realm. This dynamic of open heavens is still true today. When you find an individual or a geographic location where the heavens are open, you will often have the seer anointing activated in your life. Again, a simple prayer in these places and circumstances can activate the "eyes of your heart" or spirit to perceive or see into the spiritual realms and discern supernatural activity that is unfolding around you.

The Mount of Transfiguration

We see this principle unfold in the lives of Peter, James, and John in Matthew 17. This passage is commonly referred to as the Mount of Transfiguration.

> *Now after six days Jesus took Peter, James, and John his brother, led them up on a high mountain by themselves; and He was transfigured before them. His face shone like the sun, and His clothes became as white as the light. And behold, Moses and Elijah appeared to them, talking with Him. Then Peter answered and said to Jesus, "Lord, it is good for us to be here; if You wish, let us make here three tabernacles: one for You, one for Moses, and one for Elijah." While he was still speaking, behold, a bright cloud overshadowed them; and suddenly a voice came out of the cloud, saying, "This is My beloved Son, in whom I am well pleased. Hear Him!" And when the disciples heard it, they fell on their faces and were greatly afraid. But Jesus came and touched them and said, "Arise, and do not be afraid"* (Matthew 17:1-7).

Looking at this powerful event, we see these three disciples of Christ stepping into the spirit realm because of the open heaven that was upon Jesus. They entered into the open heaven by proximity. So what this passage really describes is an open heaven encounter. Notice that it was a specific time. This dynamic was also in operation in the first instance of an open heaven that we saw in Luke 3:21-22.

Timing is critical to opening the heavens over your life. When the disciples saw Christ transfigured, they were really seeing into the spiritual realm. Of course, this was a supernatural event; but we could also accurately define this experience by saying that the gift of discerning of spirits was activated, or we could say that the disciples had the seer anointing in operation in their lives simultaneously. They received an impartation from being in a certain place at a certain God-ordained time.

The Ascension and Open Heavens

In Hebrews 6 Jesus is described as a royal Priest according to the order of Melchizedek. He ascended. He was our forerunner; He blazed a trail into the heavenly realms. He opened up the heavens over mankind so we can enter into the spiritual realm. We can follow Christ the forerunner. That is exciting news!

> *Thus God, determining to show more abundantly to the heirs of promise the immutability of His counsel, confirmed it by an oath, that by two immutable things, in which it is impossible for God to lie, we might have strong consolation, who have fled for refuge to lay hold of the hope set before us. This hope we have as an anchor of the soul, both sure and steadfast, and which enters the Presence behind the veil, (the heavenly realms or dimensions) where the forerunner has entered for us, even Jesus, having become High Priest forever according to the order of Melchizedek* (Hebrews 6:17-20).

What does that look like? Jesus literally demonstrates passing through the heavens or going behind the veil and rising into the glory in the beginning of the Book of Acts. You see Jesus is "The Forerunner." A forerunner is a person who explores an unknown place and prepares a way for other to follow in his footsteps. A forerunner is somebody that goes ahead, making it easier for others to follow them. Jesus opened the heavens for mankind and has made a way for you and me to enter into the spiritual or heavenly realms.

> *Now when He had spoken these things, while they watched, He was taken up, and a cloud received Him out of their sight. And while they looked steadfastly toward heaven as He went up, behold, two men* [angels] *stood by them in white apparel* (Acts 1:9-10).

Jesus literally ascended into the heavens in this scripture. If we are supposed to do the same thing Jesus did, we, too, are supposed to literally ascend into the heavens. Here Jesus literally illustrates the priestly anointing or mantle of Melchizedek (Hebrews 4:14). Just as Jesus was obedient to His Father in every detail, we need to be obedient also. Sometimes God will call you to a specific place at a specific time for a specific purpose.

These previous examples are all events where the disciples had the seer anointing in operation in their lives. They are powerful examples of how the open heavens that were upon Christ impacted those who were in the same geographic area. The seer anointing was activated and strengthened in the disciples during these supernatural events.

Again, it is important to remember that the Lord can send you at a certain God-ordained time to a geographic area or specific place where the heavens are already open to help activate or open the heavens over your life. We have seen this dynamic unfold in my testimony and life. Perhaps the Lord will use a similar pattern in your life. I call this chronological and geographical obedience. Sometimes people cannot experience open heavens or get the seer anointing and all of the associated blessings activated in their lives because they are geographically disobedient.

In the next chapter I will share an amazing testimony of chronological and geographical obedience that resulted in a powerful angelic visitation. This angelic visitation served to open the heavens in a specific place and helped to accelerate the seer anointing in my life! By reading this testimony you may discover keys that can help you unlock the mysteries of the seer anointing and activate similar seer experiences in your life too.

CHAPTER 24

Chronological and Geographical Obedience and the Seer Anointing

At the Mount of Transfiguration, Jesus chose to take three of His disciples to a specific geographic location at a fixed or appointed time. There God poured out a supernatural grace to activate the seer anointing in the lives of Peter, James, and John. We see this in Matthew 17:1-2: *"Now after six days* [a specific time] *Jesus took Peter, James, and John his brother, led them up on a high mountain* [a specific place] *by themselves; and He was transfigured before them."*

Again, these are important keys to opening the heavens over your life. The disciples entered into the spirit by proximity by practicing chronological and geographical obedience.

Preach the Gospel to Every Creature

In 2006 Kathy and I were living in Kansas City, Missouri. We were experiencing wonderful supernatural encounters, angelic visitations, and great grace upon our lives and the ministry in Kansas City. In 2002, the Lord had spoken to me in a mud hut in Murchison Falls, Uganda, and instructed me to move to Kansas City and to submit to the spiritual authority of the leadership at Christ Triumphant Church. In February of 2006 the Lord spoke to me very clearly again instructing us to move to Moravian Falls, North Carolina. Quite frankly, I did not want to leave Kansas City. You see, we had grace and favor there. We were members of a wonderful fellowship, Christ Triumphant Church.

It was the first time in my life that I had a pastor who loved and fully supported the ministry. And on top of all of that, our home was free and clear of any mortgage and there was a lake in my backyard that was full of bass. You see, I love to bass fish. Sometimes the Holy Spirit goes fishing with me and tells me where to cast my line. In fact, there are even places in heaven where you can fish and swim in the rivers of God. (If you would like to read more testimonies about all of the beautiful places in heaven and what they look like, get my book *Angels in the Realms of Heaven*.)

Here is an amazing testimony. I had a pet bass named Dink who lived in my lake. I caught Dink at least six or seven times over the years that we lived on the lake. Dink had a distinctive V shape notched in his dorsal fin. I preached the Gospel to Dink the first time I caught him (*I preached to most of the bass I caught in the lake*). I explained in great detail to the fish God's simple plan of salvation. Then I asked Dink if he wanted to receive Jesus into his fishy heart, telling him to just wiggle his fins and to open his mouth three times if he wanted to be saved. He did. Then I said, "Dink, upon your confession of faith in the Lord Jesus Christ as your Lord and Savior, I baptize you in the name of the Father, in the name of the Son, and in the name of the Holy Ghost!" Then I fully submersed Dink back in the water and told him in parting, "Now go forth and **fin** no more!" After all, the Scripture encourages us to "*go into all the world and preach the gospel to **every creature**. And he who believes and is baptized will be saved*" (Mark 16:15-16, emphasis added). I just assumed that meant fish too!

"Supernatural"

Nonetheless, in obedience to the Lord, I simply told the Him, "OK, Lord; we will move, just tell us when." The Lord instructed us to prepare our home to sell and to move in 2008. Now I hope that this testimony will be encouraging to many of you who the Lord is nudging to move geographically. I call this geographical obedience. When we put our home on the market at the exact time that Lord had told us to, we received an offer to buy it even before the For Sale sign was placed in the yard! Can you say *"supernatural"*?

When we moved to Moravian Falls, the Lord instructed me to take a one-year sabbatical and to focus on building our little log cabin. He told me not to do any ministry—zero! I have to admit, it was a stretch for me and many were the late nights that I wondered if I had missed the Lord by making the move to Moravian Falls. I had promised Kathy that we would move into the new log cabin by November 27th of 2008, Thanksgiving. So I was working hard to meet that goal.

Sometimes when you are seeking to be chronologically and geographically obedient the Lord will test you.

One October night I had determined to work late. It had been a rough day. I had smashed my finger and it was throbbing; I also cut this same finger and it was bleeding on and off. The day was unusually warm, and I was sweating profusely. That day I literally poured blood, sweat, and tears into our little cabin! Kathy was visiting our family in another state. So, I decided to work as late as I could stand it in an effort to meet the deadline. I was sawing and putting up trim. I was not feeling particularly *"spiritual"* that night. I worked up until about 1:30 a.m. I accidently hit my bleeding and throbbing finger again, so I decided to call it a night.

I did not want to lose the hour and a half it would take me to drive back and forth between the cabin and the house we were renting, so I had gone to a local discount store and picked up a cheap cot and a little blanket. I pulled the temporary power and cut off all of the electricity. I took my little flashlight and my cot and settled in one of the unfinished bedrooms on the second floor. It was littered with sheetrock dust and my sweat and blood!

I took my travel Bible out and began to read the word by flashlight. I looked at the time and it was 2:30 a.m. (Psalm 23). I was totally exhausted. As I drifted off to sleep, I asked the Lord if I had missed Him by moving to Moravian Falls and building this cabin. I was not doing any ministry; and to top things off, my hands hurt, I was covered in blood, and I smelled of sweat. I thought, *Could this really be God?* This thought took the form of a *"heart prayer."*

About 4 a.m. I was startled into consciousness! Confused for a moment, I wondered if my little "heart prayer," asking the Lord if I had missed Him with the move to North Carolina, had continued; perhaps I was praying in my sleep. I awoke to discover that the manifest glory of God was suspended in the room; the reverential fear of the Lord was also hovering in that unfinished, second floor bedroom! When I opened my eyes, I saw a very bright white phosphorescent supernatural light was illuminating the room. There was no electricity, and my little flashlight was lying on the floor beside me, off. Every hair on my body seemed to stand on end, and I wondered if it were possible to crawl under the floorboards.

Parchment and Leather

Suddenly I saw a large eight-foot tall angel appear at the foot of my cot! It was the glory and glow that was coming from this angelic being that was lighting up the room. I was frozen by the angel's proximity. He was dressed in what looked to be a colonial style jacket with a big brass belt buckle and big brass buttons. This angelic being was also wearing a big hat that was adorned with a large brass looking buckle in the front. He had great big bushy eyebrows; one eyebrow was raised up at a sharp angle as he stared intently at me. In his big calloused hands was a large ledger or book of some sort. It looked to be ancient, and I thought that I could smell parchment and leather exuding from the angel's book.

This angelic messenger was glancing back and forth between the book and me with a perplexed and somewhat menacing countenance. The pages of his book were flipping by very fast like the wings of a hummingbird. I lay there for what seemed like an eternity, stunned by the presence and glory of this angelic visitor. After a few of minutes the angel took his right index finger and jammed it into the book, which stopped the pages from flipping by. The angel glanced at me again, and then I watched him scan the writing as he moved his finger down the page. After a short while he stopped and looked up at me with a twinkle in his bright green eyes.

He looked at me little more intently, as if he were trying to recognize me. I watched as his pupils focused. At that moment a welcoming smile creased his lips and his scour seemed to melt into acceptance. As the smile spread across his face, he said in a booming voice, "You are welcome here!" I did not recognize the accent that the angel spoke with. I laid there frozen by the fear of Lord and by the presence of my supernatural visitor. My eyes were now glued to the angel standing at the foot of my little cot.

I examined him carefully for about ten more seconds. His big green eyes locked with mine for an instant. A twinkle flashed in his eyes. My angelic visitor smiled at me once more, nodded his head slightly in my direction, and suddenly he vanished, leaving the glory and reverential fear of God lingering in the unfinished bedroom. After the angel had been gone for a while and the fear of the Lord subsided a little, I began to wonder if I should have asked my angelic visitor some questions. As I pondered these things in my heart, the supernatural light continued to illuminate the room for several more moments after the angel's abrupt departure. Eventually the light of the glory faded. However, I found that I was still frozen by fear in the darkness. The odor of my perspiration was now mingled with a wonderful heavenly fragrance of parchment, leather, lavender, and roses.

"Heart Prayer"

Some our friends who have stayed in that bedroom in our log home have experienced angelic encounters. I believe that the heavens were ripped open there when this angelic messenger, whom I believe to be a Moravian, stepped into the room on that warm October night. Since that time I have had literally dozens of angelic visitations in our log home in Moravian Falls. I must admit, it was nice to know that we were welcomed in the "*spirit.*" I have occasionally wondered what would have happened to someone who was not "*welcome here.*"

Perhaps the Lord released this angel as an answer to my *"heart prayer."* Remember, prayer is one of the two most important keys to opening the heavens over your life. Perhaps the Lord sent this messenger to give me revelation of the fact that God *had* positioned me in a "certain" place where the heavens were open to a greater degree. Perhaps this was the fruit of our chronological and geographical obedience. I certainly know that God releases angels and opens the heavens over peoples' lives in Moravian Falls. I could share many testimonies along this line.

On February 25, 2009, the Lord visited me at our little log home and assigned a "scribe" angel to me. Since that time I have written many books including the trilogy on angels and others with the help of this "scribe" angel. Again, this is another mysterious and glorious aspect of the Kingdom of Heaven and another of the hidden mysteries of the seer anointing. Surely God is unlocking these hidden mysteries of the seer anointing and giving them to His friends at this hour. Supernatural encounters like the one I just shared will become more and more common for you when you activate your seer gifting and learn to walk in the seer realm with maturity and wisdom.

Obedient to the Spirit

The activation or impartation of the gifts of the spirit and the seer anointing is often the fruit or outcome that unfolds in a person's life when they enter into or experience an open heaven. The last testimony shares a modern day example of this dynamic of the seer anointing activating during a supernatural experience or open heaven encounter. Let's continue by looking at additional examples and scriptural keys that can help unlock the seer anointing and open heavens. It is important to understand that many people in the Bible had their spiritual senses or the seer anointing activated to see into the realm of the spirit by stepping into places where the heavens were open. (See Genesis 32, Isaiah 6, Ezekiel 1, 2 Kings 6:17, Zechariah 2:1-5, Luke 3:21-22, Matthew 17:1-8, and Acts 1:9, to reference but a few.)

Again, it is important to remember that the Lord can send you to a geographic area or specific place where the heavens are already open to help activate or open the heavens over your life. We have seen this dynamic unfold in my testimony and life. If you read *Dancing with Angels 1,* I share a similar testimony in which the Lord sent me to Newfoundland, Canada, to activate my spiritual vision for the first time. That was the first time that I experienced a visitation of Jesus in the temporal or earthly realm. That was also the first time that I had the eyes of my understanding enlightened to see God's angels on earth (Ephesians 1:17-21).

Perhaps the Lord will use a similar pattern in your life. Sometimes people cannot experience open heavens and get the seer anointing and all of the associated blessings activated in their lives because they are geographically disobedient. One of my neighbors says it this way, "*If you are not in the place that God has called you to be you will find that there is no grace to be in the place where you are.*" I like to say that we need grace for our place! By the way, through a supernatural series of events and the grace of God we were able to finished building our log home and received our certificate of occupancy on November 17th of 2008. We enjoyed a great turkey dinner the first Thanksgiving under the open heavens in our little log home.

So allow me to encourage you to be obedient to the leadings of the Holy Spirit when you are asked to travel to a new place. Perhaps the Lord has a purpose for such a trip, and it could be something that God requires of you. Your obedience to take such a trip could turn out to be your Mount of Transfiguration experience. I call these prophetic acts of obedience. Search for places or geographic areas that are under an open heaven, and invest time seeking the Lord there. Jerusalem is a great example of a geographic place like this. I have had numerous seer experiences in the Holy City. In 2011 a fiery angel visited Kathy and I in the Ramada Inn in Jerusalem!

A geographic place where the heavens are opened can be called a Mahanaim. There are lots of places like this on the earth today. We will continue to look at other testimonies that can help you understand open heavens and how being in the right place at the right time can activate the seer gift in your life. Again, I call this chronological and geographical obedience. These are two very important keys to unlocking the hidden mysteries of the seer anointing in your life.

CHAPTER 25

Mahanaim

I call these areas where the heavens are open a Mahanaim. To me that simply means a place where God is present and where there is free or easier access into the spiritual realm. Genesis 32:2 illustrates this scriptural concept.

"When Jacob saw them [angels], *he said, 'This is God's camp.' And he called the name of that place Mahanaim."* Jacob found himself in a place (Bethel) where he experienced an angelic visitation. Jacob had a seer experience. These places are still around today, and you can find them. Let me encourage you to search them out. In 2012 we actually traveled to the genuine geographical place (Bethel) that was called Mahanaim in Genesis 32:2. We were with a group of about sixty or so people. During our time and stay at Bethel, in Israel, dozens of the people in our group experienced "seer" encounters.

I personally witnessed a stairway going up from the ground to heaven. When I saw the stairway manifest, I heard the Lord's voice saying, "Come up here." So I did. When I climbed the stairs, I came to a place in the heavenly realms to find Jesus standing with four angelic beings. The Lord spoke to me for several minutes. At the end of this experience, the Lord handed me a new weapon of spiritual warfare. It was an amazing encounter. I was surprised by the unusual free access that was inherent in the place called Bethel to enter into the heavenly realms. The land still possesses the spiritual DNA of an open heaven or Mahanaim. Many geographic places like this have a similar spiritual DNA of an open heaven or Mahanaim.

As I mentioned in the last chapter, Moravian Falls, where we are currently living, and the surrounding area is one of those kinds of places.

The disciples of Jesus were present when the heavens initially opened over the Lord on the day He was baptized; that was a Mahanaim. They saw and heard from the spiritual realm because of the open heaven that was upon Jesus. Again they experienced Christ's open heaven at the Mount of Transfiguration; that also was a Mahanaim. They were also present when the heavens opened over Christ at His Ascension; another Mahanaim. When the disciples were there by the Sea of Galilee when Jesus multiplied the bread to feed the thousands, that was a Mahanaim. When the disciples were there in Luke 5:17 *"and the power of the Lord was present to heal"* every single person, that was a Mahanaim because they witnesses and participated as the Lord worked all of those miracles. Jesus carried an open heaven within or upon Himself. God's friends can still carry an open heaven within or upon them today.

I believe that open heavens can be contagious. They can also be inherent in your spiritual DNA. Open heavens can be a generational blessing. We see this principle in Deuteronomy 28:12: *"The Lord will open to you His good treasure, **the heavens** [open heavens], to give the rain to your land in its season, and to bless all the work of your hand. You shall lend to many nations, but you shall not borrow"* (emphasis added). Such a generational blessing may play a role in the open heavens that are professed to exist in Moravian Falls, North Carolina.

The Moravians and Moravian Falls

In the early 1700s in their community lead by Count Zinzendorf in Herrnhut, Germany, the Moravians had a 24/7 prayer meeting that lasted 100 years; it began shortly after an outpouring of the Holy Spirit. Their intercession in Germany and beyond included praying for the land they purchased in the area now called the Piedmont of North Carolina, which includes Moravian Falls, named after the Moravians. It has been purported that this particular piece of land was deeded to the Lord Jesus Christ. A few years after the 100-year prayer vigil began, the Lord launched the Moravians into an amazing and effective missionary endeavor. Part of this endeavor was evangelizing the indigenous Cherokee people around Moravian Falls.

There is an unusual amount of spiritual activity in this area, and some believe open heavens exist here. I, for one, know this to be true. Personally, I believe that the open heavens that can be discerned in Moravian Falls, North Carolina, may be the fruit of the prayers of the Pentecostal Cherokee Christians who once inhabited the area.

History reveals that the Cherokee Nation had many "holy men" and spiritual leaders. Other Indian tribes considered these Cherokee "holy men" to be prophets and seers that could *see* into the future. It should be pointed out that these Cherokee seers and prophets operated in a mixture of spiritual insight and were not what Christians would consider "sanctified." However, other Indian tribes are known to have sought out these Cherokee seers for revelation. I believe that at times these Cherokee seers sought their revelation in the Moravian Falls area. I believe these Christian Cherokee seers sought the Lord in Moravian Falls at specific geographical locations. These include the two prominent knobs or peaks of the Brushy Mountains in the Moravian Falls area.

Many people today who are descendants of the Cherokees seem to have an unusually strong grace to see into the spirit. I am such a modern day Spirit-filled Cherokee, as I am 25 percent Cherokee. So, as you can imagine, this subject and this aspect of the history of Moravian Falls is near and dear to my heart. Currently I am continuing further research into these dynamics of the open heavens in Moravian Falls, and in the future I hope to write a book called *Unlocking the Hidden Mysteries of the Open Heavens in Moravian Falls*.

Moravian Falls is actually a modern day example of a Mahanaim. Perhaps open heavens are in the spiritual DNA of the very land similar to Bethel or Jerusalem in Israel. It is possible that the Lord may lead you to travel to a place that has a Mahanaim or open heaven. It has been my experience as I have spoken to many recognized seers in the Body of Christ that the Lord has often called them to move to a "specific place" or "certain place" where the seer anointing was activated in their lives (Genesis 28:11). It was also in these "certain places" where the Spirit of God helped them to massage or to activate their inherent seer gift according to the principle of Hebrews 5:14. They learned to more correctly and accurately discern both good and evil in a specific geographic place (Mahanaim or open heaven). As they were diligent to exercise their spiritual senses by reason of use, they increased the gift of the seer anointing in their lives.

I would recommend that you seek the Lord diligently with prayer and fasting, and ask Him if you should take such a "vision quest." Perhaps your geographical obedience will be the missing key to help you unlock the seer anointing in your life. Also remember to be chronologically obedient and take such a trip in the Lord's perfect timing. There are many places where you can find a Mahanaim or open heaven. Once you begin to get the heavens open over your life, you can "take" the open heaven back to your home and "water it." You can begin to exercise your spiritual senses and learn to mature in the seer realm and gifting.

Let me encourage you that the most important place that you need to get the heavens open in your life is *within your heart.* When the heavens are opened up over your life like this, *within your heart,* you will be given the grace to carry an open heaven with you any-where you go. Then you will not need to depend solely upon the anointing of the Holy Spirit and the gifts of the Spirit as you minister. When the heavens are open within your heart, the Lord will give you supernatural revelation of how you should conduct yourself. This supernatural revelation we learned earlier is the unction of the Holy Spirit. This aspect of the seer anointing can help you in both your personal life and in any ministry situations that you may find yourself in.

Many times when you carry an open heaven with or within you, the Lord will give you understanding and grace to release the glory of God into a situation or area. This is the dynamic of John 5:19: *"The Son can do nothing of Himself, but what He sees the Father do; for whatever He does, the Son also does in like manner."* I believe that Jesus, as a seer, operated in His life and ministry like this. This is the dynamic of the seer anointing that I have called the mantle of Melchizedek.

The mantle or anointing of Melchizedek is just another way of saying that we are transformed into the character of Christ. We become more like the Lord and begin to minister like He did by hearing and seeing what our Father is doing. Then you just do those things that you *see* and miracles, signs, and wonders will follow you. It is simple really. All of these wonderful blessings come from developing your relationship with the Lord. I recommend that you become diligent to develop your ability to rest in the glory of God.

The Lord once told me, "When you rest in My glory, My glory will rest upon you." This, too, is an aspect of the seer realm. Resting in the glory under an open heaven is how you develop intimacy with the Holy Spirit. The Lord will give you revelation of how you can personally cultivate the glory of God in your life and then give you the grace to release the glory to other people and places as you live under a personal Mahanaim or open heaven. These are all some of the weightier matters of the seer realms. I have written more about this kind of seer revelation in the book *Unlocking the Mysteries of the Powers of the Age to Come*. Developing intimacy and communion with the Holy Spirit are crucial to opening and maintaining open heavens over your life.

In the next chapter we will look at scriptural keys and another personal testimony that can help you understand how the glory of God and intimacy and communion with the Holy Spirit can open the heavens over your life. These keys, intimacy and communion, and cultivating the glory of God in your life can also help you maintain an open heaven and unlock the mysteries of the seer anointing in your life.

CHAPTER 26

Koinonia

If we expect to rip or rend the heavens over our lives, we must seek to enter into communion with the Holy Spirit. In late 2003 I was in British Columbia at a specific time traveling with a ministry when there was a prophetic round table for the prophets of Canada. The gentleman I was with became ill and decided he didn't want to go to the meeting in Kelowna. It was near Christmastime so everyone in our group decided they wanted to go home. No one dialogued with me about the sudden change of plans. I didn't have a home to go to; I was living out of a suitcase. I had a beautiful wife but we didn't have a home yet.

The Lord spoke to me and said, "Go ahead to Kelowna because I want to teach you something." So I went to Kelowna where there was already a room reserved for me at a beautiful resort. It was very nice. The second I walked through the door and closed it behind me, the glory and power of God came upon me and I fell down. It took me five hours to crawl to the bed. I couldn't speak a word; I could hardly think; I couldn't move. I was experiencing the powerful weighty glory of God. This went on all day, all night, and into the next day. I couldn't even get out of the bed to go to the bathroom; the glory was pressing me down into the bed. I call this kind of glory transformation glory. (For more teaching on this type of glory, get my DVD teaching *Transformation Glory*.)

Communion or Koinonia

Finally I was able to form a thought: *Lord, what are You doing?* I really thought I might die; I was experiencing the reverential fear of God in a great and mighty way. The Lord spoke to me and said, "I want to have koinonia with you." I said, "You want to have what?" I was a fairly new Christian. I didn't know what He meant. The Lord was literally speaking Greek to me!

It took me about six months of research to discover the Greek word *koinonia* in 2 Corinthians 13:14. It means to have a partnership with someone, to experience (social) intercourse with someone, to have communication back and forth freely with someone, to have communion with someone, to have fellowship or friendship with another person. That is a novel concept for many or us; to have friendship with the Creator of heaven and earth!

> *The grace of the Lord Jesus Christ, and the love of God, and the **communion** [koinonia] of the Holy Spirit be with you all. Amen* (2 Corinthians 13:14, emphasis added).

God wants to have koinonia with you. He wants to dialog with you every day. That's why Jesus came, prayed, and opened the heavens in Luke 3:21-22. He wants us to have the same relationship with God that Adam and Eve had. He restored our inheritance of open heavens. He restored our ability to have our spirit man activated. Communion with the Holy Spirit will ultimately lead to the heavens being ripped open over your life.

Christ's DNA in You

The Lord's Supper is communion with the Lord. Partaking of the Lord's Supper helps to release your spiritual DNA. When you were knit together in your mother's womb, Papa God put part of His DNA in you. When you receive Christ as your Savior, your spirit man becomes born again. When we, as born-again people, take the bread and wine (the elements) of Communion, the DNA of Jesus Christ begins to wrap around our DNA; our spiritual DNA is transformed.

You begin to step into a closer place where the mind of Christ, the nature of Christ, and the character of Christ are released in your spirit, soul, body and sphere of influence. And then you can begin to see what God is doing more easily; you can begin to hear what God is saying more clearly; you can begin to walk in what the Father has ordained for you to do more effectively. We call that an open heaven. We call that the seer anointing. God calls that your inheritance.

Melchizedek Communion and the Seer Anointing

As we take Communion, the Lord would like us to understand the supernatural way that the Lord's Supper helps to release of the mantle of Melchizedek and the seer anointing in our lives. Let's begin to investigate this scriptural mystery by looking in Genesis 13:2:

> *"Abram was very rich in livestock, in silver, and in gold."* He was prosperous. *"And he went on his journey from the South as far as Bethel, to the place where his tent had been at the beginning, between Bethel and Ai, to the place of the altar which he had made there at first. And there Abram called on the name of the Lord"* (vv. 3-5).

As we go back to Genesis 12, we have the Lord talking to Abram (later Abraham): *"Now the Lord had said to Abram: 'Get out of your country, From your family And from your father's house, To a land that I will show you'"* (v. 1). Sometimes the Lord asks us to do things, like move, and then there is a blessing that comes. When you are obedient to God, the blessing comes. If you are geographically disobedient, you can't step into the grace and favor of God that's on your life. That's important. This passage reinforces the concept of geographic and chronological obedience being linked to the supernatural release of God's blessings into your life.

God continues to decree blessings over Abram: *"I will make you a great nation; I will bless you And make your name great; And you shall be a blessing. I will bless those who bless you, And I will curse him who curses you; And in you all the families of the earth shall be blessed"*

(Genesis 12:2-3). Abram immediately began to act in obedience to God's words: "*So Abram departed as the Lord had spoken to him, and Lot went with him*" (v. 4).

When Abram and his family arrived at the exact place that God told them to go, "*The Lord appeared to Abram and said, 'To your descendants I will give this land.' And there he built an altar to the Lord* [the altar we read about in Genesis 13] *who had appeared to him. And he moved from there to the mountain east of Bethel, and he pitched his tent with Bethel on the west and Ai on the east; there he built an altar to the Lord and called on the name of the Lord*" (v. 7). Abram was chronologically and geographically obedient. When Abram arrived at the place God had called him to be, he sought to worship the Lord by giving offerings. Giving tithes, alms, and offerings are all keys that can help unlock the hidden mysteries of the seer anointing in your life. Here is a key for you: *Extravagant giving will unlock the heavens to release supernatural provision and the blessings of God into your life.*

In Genesis 32:2 we read about Abraham's grandson: "*When Jacob saw them* [angels]*, he said, 'This is God's camp.' And he called the name of that place Mahanaim.*" This was the same place Abram had built the altar in Genesis 12. It was a geographical place where God had released His blessing. It was a geographical place where the heavens were opened. Jacob received the fruit of a generational blessing that was upon his grandfather, Abram. As we discovered in the previous chapter, those blessings are the spiritual DNA of Bethel and are still active!

God Will Fight and Conquer Your Enemies

We find in Genesis 14 that some local kings had taken Abram's nephew Lot captive. When Abram heard about it, he armed his men, he divided his forces, and he pursued and attacked and ultimately conquered these enemies. "*So he brought back all the goods, and also brought back his brother Lot and his goods, as well as the women and the people*" (v. 16).

God wants us to fight and conquer our enemies like this and He wants to restore our families and everything that the enemy has stolen from us. How is that going to happen? When we come to that certain place where the heavens are open, we get that gift of discerning of spirits and the gift seer anointing working in our lives. Then we begin to see and hear from God. Then we can know the plans of God and the Lord works on our behalf to overcome our enemies. This is another great example of the fruit of the seer anointing. The seer anointing empowers you to be obedient to God because you can know His perfect will for your life. Abram's actions were prompted by the Spirit of God.

A Tithe of All

And the king of Sodom went out to meet him at the Valley of Shaveh (that is, the King's Valley), after his return from the defeat of Chedorlaomer and the kings who were with him. Then Melchizedek king of Salem brought out bread and wine; he was the priest of God Most High. And he blessed him and said: "Blessed be Abram of God Most High, Possessor of heaven and earth; And blessed be God Most High, Who has delivered your enemies into your hand." **And he gave him a tithe of all** (Genesis 14:17-20, emphasis added).

The mantle of Melchizedek can be released by giving a tithe, giving alms, or giving an offering in a similar manner that Abram did. Melchizedek (some theologians believe this was a theophany, a preincarnate visitation of Jesus Christ) *"the king of Salem* [peace] *brought out bread and wine"* (v. 18). What is that a picture of? Communion.

So when we take Communion (the Lord's Supper) there are times when we can be set free from those yokes of darkness that keep us down. There is also an anointing or aspect of the mantle of Melchizedek that increases as we take Holy Communion. These blessings of God are the open the heavens over our lives (Deuteronomy 28:12). There is a correlation between the Lord's Supper and the mantle of Melchizedek. There is a correlation between the Lord's Supper and the seer anointing. I encourage you to take the Lord's Supper every day if possible. Taking the Lord's Supper consistently is a key to unlock the seer anointing in your life. Taking the Lord's Supper consistently is a key to grow into an intimate and personal relationship with the Holy Spirit (koinonia).

There is a prophetic picture of the seer anointing in Hebrews 4. It's a prophetic picture of what God wants to do. He wants to open up the heavens in our lives and to burn out the sin and dross so that we can come boldly before the throne of grace. We can ascend into the heavenly realms like we saw Jesus do in Acts 1:9. We go vertically behind the veil where we hear, see, taste, smell, touch, and get revelation of what God is doing. And then we come back down and minister the things that we see and hear horizontally.

That's a picture of the Cross (the vertical and the horizontal). We can **do** "*Your kingdom come. Your will be done On earth as it is in heaven*" (Matthew 6:10; Luke 11:2). That is an aspect of the anointing and mantle of Melchizedek—having God's good treasure of the heavens open up over your life so that you have free access to go up, hear what Papa God says, come down, do those things you see your Father doing. Then miracles happen easily. Lives are transformed. That is walking in the fullness of God and as a mature seer. You can learn to literally pass through the heavens just like Jesus demonstrated for us.

One last point and supernatural key related to Melchizedek, Abram, Communion, and extravagant giving is that Abram gave an extravagant offering to Melchizedek. He gave Melchizedek 10 percent of the riches of seven nations. Perhaps, because of this excessive offering God released Melchizedek to decree and prophesy blessings over Abram (Genesis 14:19-20). The following scripture is the blessing given to Abram by God:

> Now the Lord had said to Abram: "Get out of your country, From your family And from your father's house, To a land that I will show you [geographical obedience]. I will make you a

great nation; I will bless you And make your name great; And you shall be a blessing. I will bless those who bless you, And I will curse him who curses you; And in you all the families of the earth shall be blessed" (Genesis 12:1-3).

It was not until Abram was obedient to go to a "certain place," a Mahanaim, that God activated His preordained destiny and blessings into Abram's life (Genesis 32:2). Abram came to a certain place at a God-ordained time, and his God-ordained DNA was activated. However, it was not until Melchizedek had blessed him that God changed who he was. He went from being Abram to Abraham, the father of many nations. These are very important keys for us to remember as we seek to uncover the hidden mysteries of the seer anointing and activate our God-ordained destiny and spiritual DNA. God can certainly change who you are (in Christ) just like He transformed Abram into Abraham. In the next chapter we will look at some final keys that can help you to activate the seer anointing in your life. These scriptural keys can also help you learn to live as a royal priest according to the order of Melchizedek enabling you to pass behind the veil and be transformed into a seer just like Christ.

CHAPTER 27

Passing Through the Heavens

Sometimes when we cannot breakthrough into the seer anointing it may be because we have soul wounds. I call those demonic yokes of darkness. As we participate in Communion, I believe there can be a release of the mantle of Melchizedek. As Melchizedek brought bread and wine and received the tithe from Abram and blessed him, we see a prophetic picture of Communion. What we see described in Genesis 14:18 is most likely Jesus Himself who was coming to foreshadow the Lord's Supper.

In Hebrews 4:14 we find: *"Seeing then that we have a great High Priest who has passed through the heavens, Jesus the Son of God, let us hold fast our confession* [of faith]." In Hebrews 5 it tells us: *"For every high priest taken from among men is appointed for men in things pertaining to God, that he may offer both gifts and sacrifices for sins. He can have compassion on those who are ignorant and going astray, since he himself is also subject to weakness. Because of this he is required as for the people, so also for himself, to offer sacrifices for sins"* (vv. 1-3). This speaks of Levitical and Aaronic priesthood.

"And no man takes this honor to himself, but he who is called by God, just as Aaron was. So also Christ did not glorify Himself to become High Priest, but it was He who said to Him: 'You are My Son, Today I have begotten You'" (Hebrews 5:4-5). What did we study earlier in Luke 3:22? God the Father spoke to Jesus and said, *"You are My beloved Son; in You I am well pleased."*

Reading on in Hebrews 5 it says, *"As He also says in another place: 'You are a priest forever According to the order of Melchizedek'; who, in the days of His flesh, when He had offered up prayers and supplications, with vehement cries and tears to Him who was able to save Him from death, and was heard because of His godly fear, though He was a Son, yet He learned* **obedience** *by the things which He suffered. And having been perfected, He became the author of eternal salvation to all who obey Him"* (vv. 6-9, emphasis added).

What was the key to releasing the blessing in Abram's life? Obedience. How did Abram become obedient? (See Hebrews 11:8.) He was able to hear God because he had developed an intimate friendship and personal relationship with Him. That's why it is critical that we have the seer anointing activated in our lives, so that we can also see and hear God well, enabling us to become obedient and move into the place where God wants us to be. As we have learned earlier, chronological and geographical obedience are keys to open the heavens, or a Mahanaim, where we can receive the mantle of Melchizedek and activate the seer anointing. In Hebrews 5:10 we find that Jesus was *"called by God as High Priest 'according to the order of Melchizedek,' of whom we have much to say, and hard to explain, since you have become dull of hearing."*

The writer of Hebrews had the revelation of Jesus as the royal Priest according to the order of Melchizedek. But the church could not understand it because they were spiritually deaf, spiritually blind, and spiritually dumb. Today God is opening up your eyes and God is opening up your ears and you are having the unction of the Holy Spirit activated within you to understand the weightier matters of the Kingdom of God. I believe as we offer our prayer to the Lord (as Abram offered tithes in Genesis 14:20) and as you partake in the Lord's Supper (take the bread and wine), there will be a release and a grace to step into the mantle of Melchizedek. This mantle or anointing is the ability to ascend into the heavenly realms. The mantle of Melchizedek is one type of the seer anointing. We will be able to discern, see, hear, taste, touch, and smell what Papa God is doing so that we can have our lives transformed. That is the seer anointing.

The mantle of Melchizedek really is just learning to become more like Christ in character and gifting.

His DNA

There is a correlation between having the heavens open up over your life and walking in sanctification. The thread that weaves through this book is the sanctifying of our spirit and soul. We need healing and deliverance from those things that are keeping us from hearing and seeing well.

We must never take the Lord's Supper lightly; we need to be in right relationship with the Lord. We all sin in some way or another, even if it's just complaining or allowing thoughts that are not pleasing to the Lord. We can pray as David did in Psalm 19:14: *"Let the words of my mouth and the meditation of my heart Be acceptable in Your sight, O Lord, my strength and my Redeemer."* Let the Holy Spirit speak to you about these things.

Ask and allow Him to take you into the past, if necessary, where you may have made unrighteous judgments or done something else that was not pleasing to God—anything that would defile your vessel or hinder or inhibit the Holy Spirit in any way from being able to fully function in and through you. When you see something, repent before God. Ask Him to forgive you and to do a deep work of cleansing and healing in your life. This is a manifestation of the seer anointing that can help bring us into a greater measure of healing, sanctification, and deliverance. Many times this kind of revelation for inner healing can come as you partake of the Lord's Supper and experience Communion.

You can take the Lord's Supper any time; you don't have to be in a corporate setting. It is a special time of communion between you and God, and it will draw you closer to Jesus. As we partake of the spiritual body and blood of the Lord, we are partaking of His DNA. The deeper we go in intimacy with the Lord, the more we can have His DNA. We have it because we are the Bride of Christ. We have to take time with the Lord to get to know His heart, His mind, and His ways. Through Communion we can be further transformed into the character and anointings of Christ.

Here is what Kathy Basconi teaches about intimacy and communion with the Lord: "We can be exactly like Jesus if we want it. We do need Him, but we also have to want Him; there's a difference. When you truly want Him, you have everything. In that place of intimacy with Him, you can keep going and going and going and never stop. In that place of intimacy, everything you need in your life will come in the greatness and in measure according to the depth that you go in intimacy and relationship with Him. It is not going before the Lord praying and asking for things; it is simply just wanting to be with Him. Out of that time invested resting in His glory comes transformation and healing. His glory and His presence come and rest upon you. His glory and His presence begin to minister to you and release healing and the spirits of wisdom and revelation. It's a beautiful supernatural exchange, it's holy."

The Fragrance of Heaven

You could say the fragrance of heaven is attached to a person who is living under an open heaven. This happened to the apostles who walked with Jesus. That can be true for friends of God today too. Some people walk under an open heaven, and you can enter into their open heavens by proximity or being around them for a time. Their open heaven can "rub off" on you.

> Now when they saw the boldness of Peter and John, and perceived that they were uneducated and untrained men, they marveled. And they realized that **they had been with Jesus** (Acts 4:13, emphasis added).

Remember, the heavens can be open over an individual as well as over a specific geographical area or location. Again, Jesus is our scriptural example for this principle concerning the dynamic of open heavens and how to enter into them by proximity. So, the Lord may lead you to submit to the ministry of a specific individual who is operating in or under an open heaven. You need to understand that certain individuals carry open heavens with them everywhere they go. You may learn from them or from their teaching materials. You may wish to consider attending events where they are ministering, teaching, or speaking. If possible, seek opportunities to interact with them on a personal basis and ask them questions. Some call this discipleship, but I prefer to call this kind of interaction friendship.

Remember, Jesus called the disciples His friends (John 15:15). I believe that is true discipleship. Although academic training in a religious institution or university is good, in my opinion it is not biblical discipleship.

The Lord used Kenneth E. Hagin to encourage and help disciple me in my early walk in the supernatural. Although I was not able to have a personal friendship with him, I was able to learn from Hagin's books and audio teachings. The Lord also used the ministry of Benny Hinn in a similar way in my life. Ask the Holy Spirit to guide you and give you direction in this area.

I hope, pray, and believe that the Lord will use this book and the other books that I have written in this way for many people to be activated in the seer anointing and to walk in the fullness of the Kingdom of Heaven.

When the heavens are open over a person or place, people will often see and hear from the realms of heaven or the spirit by proximity as the seer anointing is activated around them. You will garner supernatural revelations in such a place. We have seen this from our scriptural examples and testimonies.

This dynamic or characteristic of open heavens is still in effect today. So, I encourage you to find a place, individual, or ministry that is moving under an open heaven and then seek to invest as much time as you can in that environment. This book may well be your Mahanaim. This teaching may be used by the Lord to activate your open heaven and launch you into the seer anointing. Also, the CD set *The Seer Anointing* and the box set *The Moravian Falls School of the Seers* are available on the King of Glory website. You can listen to them over and over again until the heavens crack open over your life! Perhaps the Kingdom of Heaven will "rub off" on you. You might consider taking the free courses being offered by King of Glory Ministries International at the new International Ministry Equipping Center (iMEC). The iMEC is located in Moravian Falls. However, you can participate in the training and discipleship teachings anywhere in the world through our webcasts, archived video teachings, MP3 teachings, and other free resources on the Internet. Just visit our web page for more details.

When you enter into the proximity of an open heaven, you may begin to have the seer anointing activated in your life. At this point you are in a position to begin to exercise your spiritual senses. We need to build up spiritual senses according to the principle of Hebrew 5:14.

There is an open heaven in Moravian Falls. That is one reason why I live here. There are some folks who say that they will not stay long in this area because they get too much revelation and are not able to sleep properly. I love to be in here Moravian Falls because of the amazing way that the Lord gives me revelation and visits me in my dreams!

In conclusion, let me encourage you to seek the Lord for direction and guidance. The Holy Spirit will guide you and teach you the best methods and manner to rend the heavens over your life. You should not be in a hurry nor should you be fixated on any one avenue to "rip" or "rend" the heavens over your life. Allow the Lord to guide your steps. Some folks are not interested in traveling or ministry. God is so wonderful and kind that He gives each of us a choice of how we live out our lives. If you wish, you can choose to live a normal life with just a few of the ordinary miracles, signs, wonders, angelic visitations, and other things that happen under an open heaven.

But allow me to encourage you that you do really need to get the heavens opened over your life! You will benefit immensely from living your life under an open heaven, as the blessings of Abraham will manifest in your life. The fruit of an open heaven over your life is favor, blessing, revelation, and the release of the power, gifting, and the anointing of the Holy Spirit upon you and all that you put your hand to. You will prosper. So, I want to encourage you to rend or rip the heavens over your life.

Finally, we need to remember that it is *only* through the finished work of Jesus Christ that we can have the heavens rended or ripped open over our lives. Christ came to rend or open the heavens for all of mankind. Jesus accomplished this by His finished work on the Cross of Calvary. Therefore, we can *all* live under an open heaven today. You can learn to live with the fullness of the blessings of Abraham and the seer anointing activated in your life.

I recommend that you seek the Lord with prayer and fasting and ask Him to give you a personal revelation of how you can expect the heavens to open over your life. Ask the Lord to open the heavens within your heart. Finally, if the Lord instructs you to travel to a specific place at a specific time, be sure to be chronologically and geographically obedient. As for now, pray the prayers of activation that follow the epilog and believe to receive as you pray and seek the Lord. Perhaps you may wish to consider praying all the prayers that are written in this book each day. Seek the Lord in this, and allow the Holy Spirit to guide and teach you about the seer anointing and open heavens personally.

Epilog

On the Day of Atonement in both 2011 and 2012, I experienced two powerful encounters with the Lord in Moravian Falls, North Carolina. I document those experiences and the instructions that Jesus gave me in the book *The Sword of the Lord and the Rest of the Lord.* In fact, this book is a companion teaching to *The Sword of the Lord.*

Jesus allowed me to be taken up into the heavenly realms, and I experienced an extended seer encounter. The Day of Atonement was concluding in 2012, and heavenly aromas were lingering in the air. I had just witnessed Jesus command and deploy millions of angelic beings, as they had moved about me in the heavenly realms. I was resting in the presence and glory of God and asking Him for more revelation and understanding about the seer encounter I had just experienced.

Jesus had unsheathed His sword, and I had seen the words "The Rest of the Lord" etched into the sword of Christ. As I was pondering these experiences, I was catapulted back up into the heavenly places. I came to rest in the heavenly dimensions. Angelic worship and ethereal singing filled my ears as the glory of God again washed over my spirit, soul, and body.

Suddenly the Lord appeared in front of me once more, and Jesus was surrounded by several angelic beings. Jesus was adorned with beautiful priestly garments, and I immediately understood that the Lord was dressed in the robes and mantle of Melchizedek. This was the risen and victorious Christ. The Lord was appearing in the image of *the* royal Priest according to the order of Melchizedek. The power and authority that Jesus carried at that moment was amazing.

In the Lord's right hand, Jesus held the same sword that I had seen on the Day of Atonement in 2011 and also earlier on the Day of Atonement in 2012. The Lord's magnificent sword was reflecting the glory of God as the Lord stood there smiling at me. Perhaps I was somewhere between heaven and earth. Once again I saw etched upon the shaft of the Lord's sword were the words "The Rest of the Lord" dancing in the brilliant light of the glory realm.

In His left hand Christ held a beautifully embossed golden book that appeared to be a Bible. As I took my vision from the sword to look at the book, it began to burn brightly. Glorious blue and purple flames began to leap from the pages of the Bible in the Lord's left hand and shoot through the spiritual realm like arrows would shoot from the string of a powerful bow. Instantly I understood that the Lord was releasing revelatory knowledge and hidden mysteries to His friends at this hour. One part of this supernatural release will be the activation of the seer anointing.

I watched as these arrows of wisdom and revelation were supernaturally released into all of the earth. Innumerable angelic beings seemed to accompany each blazing heavenly arrow as they were catapulted into all the nations of the earth. I glanced at Jesus to see Him smile broadly. His smile filled my heart with joy and the knowledge that the Lord is now raising up seers and mature believers all over the earth. These friends of God will be the ones who will choose to walk in intimacy, holiness, and communion with the Lord. They will be those who are diligent to enter into the fullness of the rest of the Lord. They will be overcomers who will walk in the mantle or anointing of a royal priesthood according to the order of Melchizedek. They will be seers.

As this understanding and revelation flowed through and into me, the power and glory of God enveloped me like a tidal wave. I understood that this is exactly how God will release this end-time anointing upon the earth. The glory of God will be poured out like a flood, just as I had seen the glory of God pour out through the rip in the spiritual atmosphere on the Day of Atonement (Habakkuk 2:14; Isaiah 60:2). Nothing can stop the plans of God, and His Kingdom will come soon like a mighty spiritual tidal wave.

I was immobilized by the glory and the proximity of Jesus robed as *the* royal Priest according to the order of Melchizedek. Christ smiled at me with pleasure and joy, and I believe that I returned His smile. As I did so, there was another explosion of glory and power. Instantly the spiritual realm seemed to be rent open behind the Lord. The heavens opened.

Suddenly behind the Lord Jesus Christ were two endlessly long lines of angelic beings with mantles draped over their arms. Jesus stood with the burning word in His left hand and His sword in His right hand. There was an explosion of brilliant white light and glory, and it seemed as if seven stars were launched outward from the presence of the Lord. I understood that these stars were also going to the ends of the earth. Perhaps one of those stars represented the seer anointing. There were now thousands of angelic beings lined up in a V formation behind Jesus. I understood that these angels were all carrying mantles of anointings and weapons of spiritual warfare, like the seer anointing.

There were thousands upon thousands of these angelic beings nearby, and each one had a mantle or beautiful white robe draped over the right forearm. Instantly I understood that these angels were being released and assigned to place these mantles upon those who choose to serve the Lord fully in holiness and purity at this hour (Zechariah 3). I understood that the eyes of the Lord *are* running to and from throughout the earth seeking friends of God so that He might show Himself strong on behalf of those whose hearts are loyal to Him (2 Chronicles 16:9).

Suddenly a fiery angel appeared at the right hand of the Lord with a burst of heavenly glory and power. This angelic being was about fourteen feet tall and consisted entirely of heavenly flames of fire. Instantly the fire of God began to burn within my spirit and within my body. I began to get very hot! I thought this angel must be carrying the all-consuming fire of Almighty God (Hebrews 12:29). The reverential fear of the Lord fell upon me.

I realized that our God is a consuming fire. I also understood that the Lord is burning from His people all things that will keep us from walking in the fullness of His Kingdom and the fullness of His authority and power; that is if we allow this purging work of the Holy Spirit to set us free and cleanse us with God's healing fire (Deuteronomy 9:3). Once more I understood that when we fully trust and rest in the Lord, God Almighty will fight our battles for us. He will give us rest on every side. That is another amazing aspect of the seer anointing. It is a mantle or anointing of peace and holiness. Peace and holiness are also benefits of walking in the seer anointing and living under an open heaven.

I understood that the Lord's consuming fire is a wonderful and healing supernatural aspect of Christ's Kingdom. However, too few of God's friends are willing to submit to this ministry of the Holy Spirit and receive God's all-consuming fire. But, that is what God will require of those who would seek to walk in seer anointing at this hour. I had seen this flaming angel in Jerusalem before. It was during that visit to the Holy Land that this angel had visited me in the Jerusalem Ramada Inn. That night I awoke to see this flaming angelic being standing in the room releasing this same all-consuming fire.

Jesus was standing there with thousands upon thousands of angelic beings standing in a victory formation behind the Lord. I was astonished and wondered what I was supposed to do, because I realized that there was a response required from me at that moment. I am also certain that God will soon require a response from you.

Suddenly the flaming angel took the Bible from the left hand of Jesus and the book was transfigured into a burning scroll. It was about the size of a roll of French bread. I was mesmerized with what I was seeing. This flaming angel stood there holding the burning word, which was transformed into a burning scroll. The blue and purple flames coursing from the scroll were a perfect contrast to the brilliant colors of the fiery red and orange that were exploding from the countenance of the flaming angel of the Lord.

Then Jesus looked deeply into my eyes and said, "This is the living word" (Hebrews 4:12). I turned my gaze upon the living, burning word. I watched these beautiful purple and blue colors as they continued to boil and percolate up from the scroll.

The thought came into my mind: *Jesus is our forerunner. Jesus is the forerunner!*

Jesus said, "You must take and eat." Then Jesus smiled at me benevolently once more. At that instant the fiery angel (which I understood to be the angel of the Lord) took the flaming scroll in his flaming hands and held the scroll up for me to *"see"* clearly. Then the fiery angel bent down and placed the flaming scroll quickly into my mouth. Instantly my lips and tongue began to burn, and as I ate the scroll it tasted sweet but soon turned sour in my stomach.

As this unfolded, I understood that it is the word of God that is an all-consuming fire; and that as we are diligent to enter into the rest of the Lord, we can allow God's anointed and holy word change us. The fire of God will pierce us spirit, soul, and body. And in this way we can be transformed by the cleansing and healing fire of God. It is only by the shed blood of Messiah that we are transformed and made holy and righteous. It is only the atoning blood of Jesus Christ that can prepare us, cleanse us, and make us fit to be kings and priests before the throne of God the Father. It is only the blood of Jesus that can prepare us to receive and mantle of the seer anointing (Revelation 1:4-6; 5:6-14).

Once we reach this place, we can come boldly to the very throne of grace and allow the High Priest of our confession, Jesus Christ the Royal Priest according to the order of Melchizedek, to intercede and pray for us as individuals. It is in this place that we cease from our own work and labors and enter into the fullness of the rest of the Lord. It is in this place that we allow the Lord to intercede and to pray for us. Then we just walk out those things that we "see." This is entering into the fullness of the rest of the Lord. To walk in the mantle of Melchizedek is to discern and to understand the prayers that Jesus Christ offers up for us at the right hand of the Father. This is the ultimate manifestation of the seer anointing. I was lost in my thoughts and was pondering what this all must mean.

Then Jesus said, "It is time for my royal priesthood to arise. It is time for my people to learn to overcome the world. Tell my people that they must be diligent to enter into the rest of the Lord at this hour." Jesus was speaking to me in a parable once more!

Revelation percolated into my spirit with the understanding that the seer anointing is one of five levels of the rest of the Lord. Jesus had given me five: (1) The fullness of God's rest and the mantle of Melchizedek. (2) The Sabbath rest. (3) The heavenly hosts, the rest of God's family. (4) Resting in His glory and allowing Him to work on our behalf. (5) The hidden and mysterious treasures in the Kingdom of God.

Today I understand that the hidden and mysterious things in the Kingdom of God are revealed to God's friends through the activation of revelatory gifts such as the seer anointing. So, in a sense this book is truly a key that can help you unlock the fifth level of the rest of the Lord in your life. You can step into the hidden and mysterious dimensions of Christ's Kingdom. In fact, that is the day and hour in which we are living today. God is raising up seers, friends of God, who will help usher in the great last days harvest and the return of the King of kings and the Lord of lords, Jesus Christ of Nazareth.

When I opened my eyes, the Lord was no longer standing at my side nor was the angel of fire in my prayer room. Only the lingering fragrance of honey and roses seemed to ride upon the gently circling winds that remained. The glory and power of God was also hovering over me. Jesus has millions of mantles to give to His friends. Many of these are mantles to "see," or the seer anointing.

You can step into the mantle of Melchizedek. That simply means that you will be transformed into the character and likeness of Christ. You are called to be a seer. God will anoint your eyes with a supernatural salve that will enable you to see and to hear what the Father has ordained for you to accomplish. God promises you this in Revelation 3:18: "*I counsel you to buy from Me gold refined in the fire, that you may be rich; and white garments, that you may be clothed, that the shame of your nakedness may not be revealed; and anoint your eyes with eye salve, that you may see."* The Lord wants to anoint your eyes to see spiritually. That is the day and hour that we are living in today. You are called to "see." God wants to heal your eyes.

Once more I remembered what Jesus had told me at the Sea of Glass Like Crystal: "Tell my people to be diligent to enter into the rest of the Lord at this hour. The time has come for my people to arise. They will prophesy what they see. They shall roar like a golden lion. They will shriek like a golden eagle. When this happens the enemy will flee. Tell them the time has come to roar like a lion and to soar like an eagle—soaring to the highest heights of the heavenly realms where they will rise above the confusion and conflicts of the present world. From that place they will overcome the world and enter into My perfect will and the fullness of My rest. Tell them to soar into the heavenly realms and see what must take place after this."

It's time for the Body of Christ to "soar and roar."

It's time for the Body of Christ to "see and decree."

Amen.

Prayer of Activation

Rest in the Lord and seek Him in prayer. Allow the Spirit of God to minister to you. When you are ready, pray the following prayer of activation; simply purpose in your heart that you will "believe to receive." No one has to "lay hands" on you. You can receive a supernatural activation from the realms of heaven and directly from the Spirit of God.

When you are spiritually prepared and feel ready rest in a comfortable place and prepare to receive an activation to see, pray the following prayer out loud and then rest in the presence of the Lord and begin to exercise your spiritual senses.

> *Lord, I come to You; I want to be like You. I do need You, Lord; but more than that I want You. Forgive me, Lord. Bring me to that high and holy place with You. Thank You for the Cross. Thank You for all You did for me, God. It's beautiful; it's holy. I bless Your holy name.*

> *Holy Spirit, I do invite You and I honor You. Father, I thank You for the Holy Ghost. Lord, I thank You that the heavens are open and I ask that you would come and minister to me. Lord, I don't understand everything; I don't need to. I ask that You would release that mantle of Melchizedek, that ability to ascend into the heavenly realms, that ability to come boldly*

before the throne of grace. I ask that You would release the Abrahamic blessing to me.

Father, I thank You for healing me, restoring my soul. Thank You that You are preparing me—my mind, my body, my heart—to receive what You are going to do in and with me. I give You all the praise and the honor and the glory.

Jesus, You told me to ask. You told me to seek. You told me to knock. I'm now constraining You, Lord; I'm asking, I'm seeking, I'm knocking. I thank You that You are opening up doors and I'm going to step into the Kingdom of God; I'm going to have my eyes opened so I can see and my mind so I can understand Your Kingdom.

Lord, I welcome You. Holy Spirit, You are welcome to come and dwell within me to guide me and to teach me. Father, I thank You that You are releasing the unction of the Holy Spirit into my life. Lord, I give You all the praise and the honor and the glory for everything You are going to do in my life as I receive this impartation. I thank You, Father God, that the Kingdom of God is already within me and that You are going to activate my DNA. I thank You, Lord, that when I took the Lord's Supper, the DNA of Jesus wrapped around my DNA and I'm being transformed. My mind is being transformed and my spiritual eyes are opening.

I speak to every demon from hell; I say, "Loose me now!" I cover myself with the blood of Jesus and I say, "Lord, I'm prepared! I'm ready! And I ask for activation. I ask for impartation." Lord, You said if we, being evil, know how to give good gifts, how much more will our heavenly Father give the Holy Spirit to those who ask. So, Holy Spirit, I am asking for You to come. You are the one who gives gifts and I'm asking that You would release the gift of wisdom and revelation in my life. Activate the gift of discerning of spirits in my life today, Lord.

O Lord, open my spiritual eyes and let me come to a place like Jacob that I can call the camp of God. Lord, open my eyes and let me find Mahanaim. Lord, I ask for intimacy and communion with Your Spirit. Jesus, manifest Yourself and Your Kingdom to me. Lord, let me really know You. Let me see Your face. Lord, let Your Kingdom come. Lord, open my eyes to see Your Kingdom here on earth as it is in heaven.

Holy Spirit, I thank You, I praise You, I give You honor and glory. Lord, I ask that as I wait upon Your presence that You would begin to give me grace to receive.

Now pause a moment and receive. Focus on the Lord. Take some time to wait on the Lord and allow the Holy Spirit to teach you. Let the Lord lead you and go with what the eyes of your heart start to see. You don't have to fall down; you don't have to hear thunder; you don't have to feel lightening. Only believe to receive. Now take some time to rest in the glory and presence of the Holy Spirit and invite the Lord to open your eyes to "see and hear" what must take place after this, as it tells us in Revelation 4:1-11:

After these things I looked, and behold, a door standing open in heaven. And the first voice which I heard was like a trumpet speaking with me, saying, "Come up here, and I will show you things which must take place after this."

Immediately I was in the Spirit; and behold, a throne set in heaven, and One sat on the throne. And He who sat there was like a jasper and a sardius stone in appearance; and there was a rainbow around the throne, in appearance like an emerald. Around the throne were twenty-four thrones, and on the thrones I saw twenty-four elders sitting, clothed in white robes; and they had crowns of gold on their heads.

And from the throne proceeded lightnings, thunderings, and voices. Seven lamps of fire were burning before the throne, which are the seven Spirits of God. Before the throne there was a sea of glass, like crystal. And in the midst of the throne, and around the throne, were four living creatures full of eyes in front and in back.

The first living creature was like a lion, the second living creature like a calf, the third living creature had a face like a man, and the fourth living creature was like a flying eagle.

The four living creatures, each having six wings, were full of eyes around and within. And they do not rest day or night, saying: "Holy, holy, holy, Lord God Almighty, Who was and is and is to come!"

Whenever the living creatures give glory and honor and thanks to Him who sits on the throne, who lives forever and ever, the twenty-four elders fall down before Him who sits on the throne and worship Him who lives forever and ever, and cast their crowns before the throne, saying: "You are worthy, O Lord, To receive glory and honor and power; For You created all things, And by Your will they exist and were created."

Prayer of Salvation

Perhaps you would like to be born again and receive Jesus as your Lord and Savior now. Just pray this prayer out loud:

Father God, I believe that Jesus Christ is the Savior or Messiah. I believe that Jesus is the only begotten Son of God and that He died upon the Cross to make payment for my sins. I believe that Jesus was buried in an unused grave, but that after three days He rose again to conquer death and sin. Lord, because I was born a human being, I was born a sinner. Lord, I ask you to forgive my sins now in the name of Jesus Christ of Nazareth. God, cover my sins with the atoning blood of Jesus and forgive me now. I receive Jesus Christ as my Savior and Lord. Amen.

Daily Prayer of Activation

At this moment I bless my God and the Father of my Lord Jesus Christ, who has blessed me with every spiritual blessing in the heavenly places in Christ. And I pray that the God of my Lord Jesus Christ, the Father of glory, may give unto me the spirit of wisdom and revelation in the knowledge of Him. Lord, I ask in the name of Jesus Christ of Nazareth that the eyes of my spirit might receive supernatural understanding and become enlightened.

I ask, Father, that I may know what is the hope of Your calling upon my life and comprehend what are the riches of the glory of the Lord's inheritance in me. Lord, reveal to me what is the exceeding greatness of Your power toward me, because I believe. Lord, release to me the revelatory understanding according to the working of Your mighty power which You worked in Christ Jesus as He rose from the dead and You seated Him at Your right hand in the heavenly places.

Father, You placed the Lord Jesus far above every principality and power and might and dominion and every name that is named, not only in this age but also in that which is to come. Lord, make known to me all of the fullness and unsearchable riches of Christ. Help me to see and comprehend what is the fellowship of the mystery, which from the beginning of the ages has been hidden in God who created all things through Jesus Christ.

For this reason I bow my knees to the Father of our Lord Jesus Christ from whom the whole family in heaven and earth is named. And I ask You, Lord, that You would grant unto me according to the riches of His glory, that I may be strengthened with might through Your Spirit in my soul and inner man. Lord, I pray that Christ may dwell in my heart through faith; that I will become rooted and grounded in the love of God.

Lord, I ask that I might comprehend with all the saints what is the width and length and depth and height—and to personally know and experience the love of Christ, which passes all knowledge, that I may be filled with all the fullness of God. And I thank You, Lord, as You are able to do exceedingly abundantly above all that I can ask or think, according to the power of Your Spirit that works within me.

Lord, I thank You now that You are releasing to me the spirit of wisdom and revelation of Your Kingdom and the mighty effectual working of your power in my life—spirit, soul, and body. Thank you, Lord, that You are opening the eyes of my heart and helping me to see and discern the fullness of your Kingdom as it manifest in my life. And to You, Lord, be all the glory in the church by Christ Jesus to all generations forever and ever. Amen.

Prayer for the Cleansing of the Heart

In Jesus name I thank You, Father, for everything You are doing. And, Lord, I thank You that You give Your children good gifts. I thank You that if I seek Your Kingdom, You will give me revelatory knowledge. Lord, I know that when I seek to have my eyes and ears activated, You will not give me a stone or a scorpion; You will give me the Kingdom of God. In the name of Jesus Christ of Nazareth, I am asking You for Your good gifts. I am asking that You open up my eyes to see and open up my ears to hear. Lord, forgive me if I have allowed prophecy, prophets, or other spiritual gifts to become idols in my heart. I repent for these things now.

Lord, I ask You to search my heart. I ask that You would take from me idols of fear, idols of unbelief, idols of doubt, or un-Christlike beliefs that might dominate my heart. Show me any areas, any hidden agendas within my heart, that are not in tune with You and that would hinder me from hearing You clearly, God. I ask that You would reveal them to me. Show me anything that would inhibit me from receiving the fullness of the anointing to see, any hindrance or roadblock that would keep me from stepping into the fullness of Your Kingdom.

Bring to my remembrance anything that would prevent me from entering into the deep things of God. If I have made unrighteous judgments against others or if the words of my mouth or the meditations of my heart have been unacceptable in Your sight, Lord, I ask that You would reveal them to me now. As I wait on You, Lord, and You show me the areas where I have sinned or fallen short, I ask that You would minister to me. By Your grace I do repent of those things with all of my heart. Please forgive me, Lord. Forgive me of strongholds or anything in my heart that is unacceptable to You. I beg You to create in me a clean heart and renew a steadfast spirit within me. Restore my soul. I thank You that You are setting me free. Lord, I ask You to cover me in Your blood. Your word says in Isaiah 43:26 that if we put You in remembrance that You will contend with us. Your word says in Revelation 1:5-6 that the blood of Jesus makes us kings and priests. Lord, I thank You for the miracle of my purification. Lord, I thank You that You are preparing me to step into the fullness of the seer anointing. I give You all the praise and the honor and the glory for all that You are doing. I pray as King David did in Psalm 51:10, "Create in me a clean heart, O God, And renew a steadfast spirit within me."

Lord, I position myself to receive from the realms of heaven. I ask, Holy Spirit, that You would begin to speak to me. I thank You, Lord, that You are activating my ability to see and hear and taste and smell and touch and enter and inherit the Kingdom of God. I ask that You activate the gift of the seer anointing in my life. In the name of Jesus Christ of Nazareth, I pray. Amen.

Offensive Prayer

Father, I thank You that there is no weapon that is formed against me that shall prosper. Every tongue that is risen against me—incantations or word curses of witchcraft—I condemn. I command every religious spirit and every demon assigned to these word curses to loose your assignments immediately, in the mighty name of Jesus Christ of Nazareth. I bind every word curse that that has been spoken against me, and I condemn them now, because this is my authority and my inheritance as a servant of the Most High God. Amen!

Recommended Reading

For further study and understanding, we recommend these books:

The Sword of the Lord and the Rest of the Lord
    —Kevin Basconi

31 Word Decrees That Can Revolutionize Your Life
    —Kevin Basconi

Unlocking the Hidden Mysteries of the Powers of the Age to Come
    —*Kevin Basconi*

The Reality of Angelic Ministry Today trilogy:

Dancing With Angels1:
How You Can Work With the Angels in Your Life
    —Kevin Basconi

Dancing With Angels 2:
The Role of the Holy Spirit and Open Heavens in Activating Your Angelic Visitations
    —Kevin Basconi

Dancing With Angels 3:
Angels in the Realms of Heaven
    —Kevin Basconi

The Apostle Paul: His Supernatural Walk With Jesus
    —KEVIN BASCONI—COMING SOON

Come Up Higher
    —PAUL COX, ASLAN'S PLACE

I Believe in Jesus
    —KENNETH E. HAGIN, KENNETH E. HAGIN MINISTRIES

Love the Way to Victory
    —KENNETH E. HAGIN, KENNETH E. HAGIN MINISTRIES

The Name of Jesus
    —KENNETH E. HAGIN, KENNETH E. HAGIN MINISTRIES

Good Morning Holy Spirit
    —BENNY HINN, THOMAS NELSON PUBLICATIONS

Secrets of the Argentine Revival
    —EDWARD R. MILLER, PENIEL PUBLICATIONS

Open My Eyes Lord
    —GARY OATES, ROBERT LAMB, RANDY CLARK,
OPEN HEAVEN PUBLICATIONS

Churchquake
    —C. PETER WAGNER

School of the Seers
    —JONATHAN WELTON, DESTINY IMAGE PUBLISHERS

Angels on Assignment
    —ROLAND BUCK, WHITAKER HOUSE PUBLICATIONS

Angels: Knowing Their Purpose Releasing Power
    —CHARLES CAPPS

About the Author

King of Glory Ministries International is all about the commission of Jesus Christ. The words of Isaiah 61 can be used to concisely summarize the call of the ministry.

> *The Spirit of the Lord GOD is upon Me, Because the Lord has anointed Me To preach good tidings to the poor; He has sent Me to heal the brokenhearted, To proclaim liberty to the captives, And the opening of the prison to those who are bound; To proclaim the acceptable year of the LORD, And the day of vengeance of our God; To comfort all who mourn, To console those who mourn in Zion, To give them beauty for ashes, The oil of joy for mourning, The garment of praise for the spirit of heaviness; That they may be called trees of righteousness, The planting of the Lord, that He may be glorified (Isaiah 61:1-3).*

Kevin and Kathy Basconi have sought to preach the Gospel of the Kingdom to the lost in many nations. As of this writing, we have visited thirty-three nations and five continents to proclaim the truth of Christ's total salvation and healing message or the Gospel of the Kingdom that Jesus instructed His disciples to proclaim. (See Matthew 4:23; 9:35; 24:14.) We have preached to hundreds of thousands of people and seen tens of thousands make the decision to receive Jesus Christ as Lord and Savior. We continue to minister in Gospel outreaches as opportunity allows and as the Spirit leads.

Kevin and Kathy also minister in churches, King of Glory Ministries International Schools, and conference meetings in various nations. They have also begun to develop the King of Glory Ministries International (iMEC); International Ministry Equipping Center in Moravian Falls, North Carolina. For more information about the (iMEC) visit our web page.

The other critical calling of King of Glory Ministries International is to minister the love of the Father to widows and orphans. This humanitarian aspect of our call can be defined in the scriptures of James 1:27 and Psalm 68:5. James 1:27 tells us this: "Pure and undefiled religion before God and the Father is this: to visit orphans and widows in their trouble, and to keep oneself unspotted from the world." God has birthed in Kevin and Kathy a heart to minister in deed and not word alone. We also see this aspect of the Father's heart in Psalm 68:5: "A father of the fatherless, a defender of widows, Is God in His holy habitation." (See the Orphanage Tab on ministry's web page for more information about this important aspect of King of Glory Ministries International.)

The ministry is punctuated by many miracles, healings, and signs and wonders that confirm the word of God. They live in the mountains of North Carolina where they pursue a lifestyle of intimacy with Jesus. Kevin is an internationally published author and artist. He the author of several books, including *The Sword of the Lord and the Rest of the Lord* and the trilogy, *The Reality of Angelic Ministry Today*. Kevin has been graced by God to see into the spiritual realm for over a decade. Kevin is also called to equip the church to operate in the seer anointing and to understand how to enter into the presence and glory of God. Kevin is an ordained minister accredited with World Ministry Fellowship of Plano, Texas. King of Glory Ministries International is connected to the apostolic leadership of Pastor Alan and Carol Koch of Christ Triumphant Church located In Lee's Summit, Missouri.

Contact the Author

Kevin and Kathy would love to hear your testimonies
about how this book has impacted your walk with Christ.
To submit testimonies contact them by e-mail.
info@kingofgloryministries.org

King of Glory Ministries International
is available to teach the material covered in this book
in much greater depth in our
School of the Seers—Level One and Level Two

These schools are also available in DVD and CD formats.

For more information or to order additional books
And other resources visit our web page at:

www.kingofgloryministries.org
Email: info@kingofgloryministries.org.
Phone: 336-818-1210 or 828-320-3502

Mailing Address:
King of Glory Ministries International
PO Box 903, Moravian Falls, NC 28654

Prophetic Worship CD

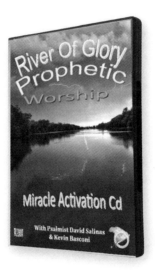

This worship Cd, *River Of Glory Prophetic Worship*, was recorded live on Saturday, November 2nd, 2014 at Christ Triumphant Church. (All sales benefit widows and orphans). We believe that the glory that was present in this session is attached to this digitally re-mastered recording. Psalmist David Salinas ushered in the glory of God during the worship in this meeting. Then Kevin was actually taken up into the throne room. Kevin began to decree the things that he was seeing in the heavenly realms. We believe that as Kevin decrees the supernatural things that he witnessed in the Throne room on this Mp3, you can also receive your miracle and healing as you listen and soak to the worship and spontaneous decrees of heaven.

~~$19.99~~

SALE $12.00

Activating Your
20/20 Spiritual Vision CD

In this message, *Activating Your 20/20 Spiritual Vision*, Kevin shares several keys that can help you to establish your seer gift and your 20/20 spiritual senses. It is imperative the we become diligent to hear the voice of the Lord and to see what God is doing in our lives at this hour. It is imperative the you develop and build up your ability to discern both good and evil each and every day according to the principle of Hebrews 5:14; Solid food belongs to those who are mature, those who by reason of use have their senses exercised to discern both good and evil. God is seeking to heal and open the spiritual eyes and spiritual ears of His people at this hour. We believe that this message and the prayer of impartation at the end can help spark such a supernatural metamorphosis in your life too! You can learn to discern and activate your 20/20 spiritual senses and vision enabling you to recreate Christ in your sphere of influence. Amen!

~~$12.00~~

SALE $10.00

Apostolic Love
CD

This digitally mastered Cd teaching outlines your right and ability to become a royal priest after the order of Melchizedek. The Blood is Jesus Christ and the Apostolic Love of God opens this door to the heavenly realms to each of us.

$12.00

SALE $10.00

Moravian Falls School Of The Seers Box Set 8 CD

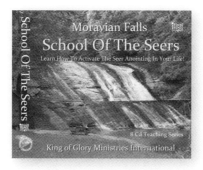

This 8 cd box set is designed to empower you to activate the seer anointing in your life. God created each of us in His image, and as such our spiritual DNA is designed to see and to be seers. We are created to have intimacy and communion with God. We are created to see and hear the Lord clearly. These teaching will help you to activate your ability to hear and see from the realms of heaven clearly. When you activate your seer gifting it can be life changing! This set includes these teachings by Kevin & Kathy Basconi:

Lesson #1 - Disc #1 - What Is The Seer Anointing Lesson #1 - Disc #2 - What Is The Seer Anointing Part #2 Lesson #2 - Disc #3 - Understanding The Seer Anointing Lesson #2 - Disc #4 - Understanding The Seer Anointing Part #2 Lesson #3 - Disc #5 The Seer Anointing & The Gift of Discerning Of Spirits Lesson #4 - Disc #6 The Seer Anointing & Open Heavens Lesson #5 - Disc #7 Activating the Seer Anointing - Part #2 Lesson #5 - Disc #8 Prayers of Impartation To Receive The Seer Anointing - Part #2

~~$85.00~~

SALE $65.00

Cultivating The Glory
3 DVD School

This 3 DVD School set is designed to help you understand and activate the glory of God to work in your life. Understanding how to live in the glory realms can transform your life! In these teaching DVDs Kevin shares amazing testimonies of supernatural encounters with God's tangible Shekinah glory!

$29.99

SALE $24.00

Sowing into the Glory
DVD

In this DVD teaching Kevin shares another powerful testimony about how you can activate supernatural prosperity in your life and circumstances when you learn to Sow Into The Glory! This message was birthed when Kevin experienced an extended season and visitation of God's glory. The Lord also allowed Kevin to understand how God releases powerful angels from the heavenly realms to help empower those who are seeking to further His kingdom. This dynamic is one aspect of the mantle or anointing of Melchizedek that the Lord is releasing to His friends at this hour. Kevin and Kathy experienced an extraordinary angelic visitation on Sunday, April 29th, 2012. When this angel of the Lord manifested so did a tangible purple glory cloud. In that atmosphere of God's glory, creative miracles began to occur, and over the course of the next year Kevin was given revelation about these Kingdom principles in relationship to supernatural provision and creative miracles.

$15.00

SALE $12.00

The Powers Of The Age To Come
& The Glory Of God CD

This message, *The Powers Of The Age To Come & The Glory Of God* was birthed in revival. Learn to live in the power of God, in God's Love, and with Gods healing and redeeming power in your life and in your sphere of influence! Learning about the powers of the age to come is crucial for every believer today. Our prayer is that this message will help you to step into the greater works of John 14:10-12, and activate the power of the age to come in your life.

~~$12.00~~

SALE $9.00

Discerning & Overcoming
The Accuser of the Brethren CD

This 2 Cd message, *Discerning & Overcoming The Accuser of the Brethren*, can transform your life through the anointed Word of God! The anointing breaks the heavy yokes and burdens of darkness and deception. You can learn to set yourself free from yokes of darkness and oppression and as you do your life will be transformed! You can go from hopelessness to hope, from sickness to health, from poverty to prosperity.

$12.00

SALE $9.00

The Sword of the Lord
& The Rest of the Lord

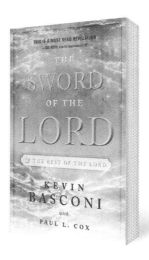

This book *The Sword of the Lord & The Rest of the Lord* was birthed on the Day of Atonement in 2011 and completed on the Day of Atonement in 2012.

Kevin was taken up into the heavenly realms and began to see a tremendous storm full of ominous black clouds moving across the horizon. After some time Kevin witnessed the sky split open and saw the Lord Jesus Christ decent towards the earth upon a mighty white stallion. Jesus was accompanied by millions upon millions of angelic beings who were arrayed for battle. The Lord of Hosts and these millions of angels began to confront the darkness and the billowing storm below. This book is a vivid depiction of those events.

Co-Authored with Paul Cox.

~~$20.00~~

SALE $15.00

Unlocking the Hidden Mysteries of the Seer Anointing

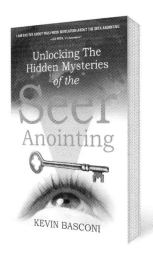

This book contains the teachings the revelations that the Lord has given Kevin over the last 12 year about the seer anointing. We are living in a God ordained moment of time when the seer realm is being released by grace to God's friends (whosoever). This book is designed to help God's people unlock the hidden mysteries of the seer anointing in their lives by understanding the idiosyncrasies of the seer anointing in a Christ centered and sound biblical manner. It is a very through biblical teaching that also is replete with dozens of prayers of activation for the reader (seers).

~~$20.00~~

SALE $15.00

This book was prepared for printing by

King of Glory Printing & Publishing

Our goal is to help unpublished authors facilitate printing of their manuscripts in a professional and economical way. If you have a manuscript you would like to have printed, contact us:

336-818-1210
or
828-320-3502

PO BOX 903
Moravian Falls, NC 28654

www.kingofgloryministries.org